books designed with giving in mind

Kid's Pets Book	The Compleat American	Working Couples
Make It Ahead	Housewife 1776	Mexican
French Cooking	Low Carbohydrate Cookbook	Sunday Breakfast
Soups & Stews	Kid's Cookbook	Fisherman's Wharf Cookbook
Crepes & Omelets	Italian	Charcoal Cookbook
Microwave Cooking	Cheese Guide & Cookbook	Ice Cream Cookbook
Vegetable Cookbook	Miller's German	Hippo Hamburger
Kid's Arts and Crafts	Quiche & Souffle	Blender Cookbook
Bread Baking	To My Daughter, With Love	The Wok, a Chinese Cookbook
The Crockery Pot Cookbook	Natural Foods	Cast Iron Cookbook
Kid's Garden Book	Chinese Vegetarian	Japanese Country
Classic Greek Cooking	Jewish Gourmet	Fondue Cookbook

from nitty gritty productions

A special "thank you" from the author to:

My four children, Jerry, Bill and Dana, who enjoy good food, and Jay, who complains - which is helpful too;

A patient husband, Bill, Sr.;

A talented artist, Craig Torlucci, who developed a style uniquely suited to the subject matter of this book;

Pamela Borges, for her helpful advice as one-half of a working couple;

Kip, Eric, Patricia, Ralph, Renato, Eveanne, and all my other friends who gave so generously of their favorite recipes and their time;

Mike Nelson, who struggled valiantly (and successfully!) to put together the unusual layout necessary for those who use this book;

Earl Goldman, who insisted I complete the task;

And to all the "Working Couples" who made the writing of this book so timely and necessary.

Working Couple's cookbook

By Peggy Treadwell

Illustrations by Craig Torlucci

Table of Contents

Working Couples

The Working Couples cookbook is designed to facilitate cooperative meal preparation by two people. In most cases, the couple will be husband and wife; however, the book will be just as helpful for any two people, be they roommates, soulmates, playmates, or wedded mates.

The "his" and "hers" divisions of culinary duties are, of course, interchangeable and could as easily be designated his and his or hers and hers.

Let's face it — when you both work, you are both tired when you arrive home. Tired and hungry. What better way to solve the ever-constant problem of who is going to prepare the meal than to prepare it together. This way, the process of preparation becomes fun, creative and a mutually satisfying venture . . . satisfying psychologically, as well as gastronomically!

The clean-up duties should also be shared and duties such as clearing the table, rinsing and stacking the dishes, disposing of the garbage and all the other details of clearing up can be interchanged. This is part of the kitchen routine — most people feel it is the most distasteful part — but this too can be made easier through cooperation of both people.

This book has been divided into three major sections: Quick 'N Easy menus for the preparation at the end of the work day, normally Monday through Friday; a Foreign Night In section for those nights when you feel like spending a little more time preparing dinner, and want the authenticity of a meal from one of your favorite countries; and the Weekend Gourmet section when you have more time available to expand your talents, and enjoy a gourmet dinner prepared by the two of you, for the two of you.

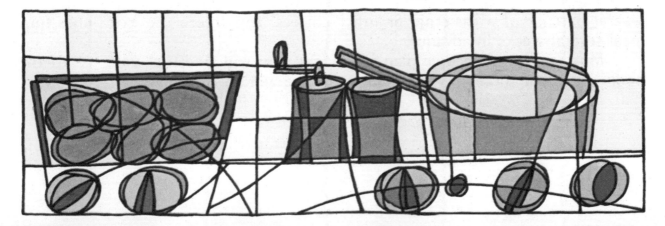

Plan and Shop Ahead

The best way to use this book, and to avoid the problem of deciding what you are going to have for dinner just before you prepare it, is to plan your entire week's menu in advance. Then, when you go shopping, you can purchase the ingredients for the week, and they will be waiting for you in the refrigerator or freezer when you arrive home from work.

Don't hesitate to change menus in the book if they contain food items that don't agree with your palate. Just cross out our suggestions, and write in your own, so that the book will be truly yours.

The working couple should use their freezers wisely. Often, you can make several batches of a casserole or other entrees, and freeze the extra ones for a meal several weeks in advance.

Most successful people plan ahead, and you will find that your use of this book, and your success as a cooking twosome will be the greatest if you do.

When Company Arrives

If you are the type of couple that often invites friends over, and frequently does so on a spontaneous basis, you can still use this book, although it was not specifically planned for that purpose.

Every recipe in the Working Couples cookbook is designed for just two people, however you can simply double, triple, or even quadruple all of the recipes herein, and accommodate your guests with ease.

This makes it possible for cooperative cooking to also be cooperative company cooking. Your guests will be pleased to know that the two of you work together on the dinner, and who knows, you may help create another convert to the working couples cooperative cooking club.

It's always fun if both of you get into the act when it comes to serving the dinner also. One of you can toss the salad at the table, just like the chef in the famous restaurants do, while the other one serves up the entree, or pours the wine. This way the serving goes faster, and the work is shared.

The whole theory behind the Working Couples cookbook is that it's only fair for both of you to help prepare and serve the dinner if you both have to work to earn the money to pay for the ingredients.

This section of the Working Couples cookbook is designed for weekday evening meals. The menus utilize convenience foods along with some dishes prepared from basic ingredients. Feel free to substitute in the menus, omit desserts, add your own special touches to the recipes, always keeping in mind your partner's tastes and abilities.

I have purposely not specified "minutes per step" for the simple reason that some people chop vegetables fast and some chop them very slowly. We work at different speeds. Therefore, the directions may say "When partner places casserole in oven, begin preparation of the vegetable." Hopefully, this will reduce pressure on the individual preparing the casserole, knowing that the timing begins when it is in the oven.

Quick 'n Easy

1

BROILED T-BONE STEAKS
TOASTED ENGLISH MUFFINS
GREEN SALAD WITH ROQUEFORT DRESSING
CHERRIES JUBILEE

HIS

1. Preheat broiler.
2. Prepare steaks for broiling: trim, butter, and add garlic if you wish.
3. Broil steaks according to individual preference.
4. Set table. (Candles are a nice touch!)
5. Open can of pie filling and place in saucepan to heat. When just beginning to bubble, turn off heat and cover.
6. Serve steaks. Partner will add toasted muffins to plates.

2

Entree: 2 T-bone steaks
          1 T butter
          Garlic (optional)
Salad: Lettuce, cucumber, celery, endive
          Roquefort dressing
Bread: 2 English muffins
Dessert: 1 can cherry pie filling
          2 scoops vanilla ice cream
          2 T kirsch

HERS

1. Prepare salad greens and place on individual salad plates or bowls.
2. Put dressing in small bowl and place on table.
3. When steaks are almost done, toast the muffins and butter them while they are still warm. Place on dinner plate with the steaks. (Fresh parsley garnish with the steaks is a nice touch if you happen to have any on hand.)
4. To serve Cherries Jubilee: Heat cherry pie filling again briefly, place ice cream in serving dishes, top with pie filling, add 1 T kirsch to each dish and flame.

(This is a Quick and Easy meal for a weekday SPECIAL OCCASION!!)

3

STEAK DIANE
BEEF RICE-A-RONI
GARLIC CHERRY TOMATOES
CITRUS CUP

HIS

1. Set table.
2. Wash tomatoes, drain on paper towel.
3. Crush garlic clove.
4. Melt butter in skillet over low heat, add garlic and saute just a bit; add tomatoes and heat, stirring often so all contents of pan become coated with butter. (This takes about 5 minutes.)
5. Sprinkle with salt and pepper and serve.
6. Serve dessert.

Entree:	1 sirloin steak (about 2 lbs)	1 t Worchestershire sauce
	1 cube butter	Salt and pepper
	1 t chives	
Vegetables:	12 cherry tomatoes	
	1 garlic clove	
	Salt and freshly ground pepper	
Rice:	1 pkg beef Rice-a-roni	
	16 oz can mushroom gravy	
Dessert:	1 orange	1 T honey
	1 grapefruit (pink, if available)	3 T shredded coconut

1. Prepare Rice-a-roni, adding mushroom gravy when 5 minutes remain on timer.
2. Peel fruits, section and arrange in dessert dishes.
3. Drizzle 1 tsp honey over each serving and sprinkle with coconut. Refrigerate.
4. Trim fat from steak; season with salt and freshly ground pepper.
5. Melt butter in large skillet. When partner puts the cherry tomatoes in a skillet, bring your pan to high heat and sear the steak on each side for 2 - 3 minutes and serve.
6. Serve Rice-a-roni.

HERS

STEAK SLIVERS ON RICE
PEAS IN BUTTER SAUCE
ENGLISH TOFFEE ICE CREAM A CREME DE COCOA

HIS

1. Chop onion and slice tomato.
2. Cut steak into thin strips, place in bowl and dust with flour.
3. Add soy sauce and toss lightly in bowl.
4. When partner starts to prepare rice, cook peas according to package directions.
5. Set table.
6. Serve peas.
7. Serve dessert when entree has been thoroughly enjoyed.

Entree:	1 1/2 lb top round steak	1 clove garlic
	2 T cooking oil	1 onion
	1 fresh tomato	1 T flour
	1 T soy sauce	1 T brown sugar
	2 T red wine	
Rice:	2 cups instant rice	
Vegetable:	1 pkg Green Giant peas in butter sauce	
Dessert:	1 pint English Toffee ice cream	
	4 T Creme de Cocoa	

1. Heat oil in heavy skillet and slice garlic clove into pan.
2. Saute onion until soft.
3. Add beef strips and saute until lightly browned.
4. Add tomato and simmer for 5 minutes.
5. Add brown sugar and wine, reduce heat to low and cover. Simmer for 15 minutes. (Set timer!)
6. Prepare 2 servings of minute rice. (Remind partner to start peas.)
7. Serve beef strips and sauce over rice.

HERS

7

BEEF STEW STROGANOFF
FRENCH ROLLS
CHERRY TOMATOES AND CELERY STALKS
FRUIT DESSERT

HIS

1. Preheat oven to 300°.
2. Place frozen fruit in pan of hot water to thaw.
3. Open cans of beef stew and mushrooms.
4. Drain mushrooms.
5. In a 3-quart saucepan, melt 1 T butter; add mushrooms and saute.
6. Add beef stew. Heat thoroughly, stirring occasionally.
7. While stew is heating, put rolls on a cookie sheet and place in oven.
8. Wash cherry tomatoes; wash and trim celery.
9. Stir 1/4 cup sour cream into the stew and heat - do not boil.
10. Serve everything and accept your partner's compliments graciously.
11. Open pkgs of fruit and combine in dessert dishes by alternate spoonsful.

Entree: 1 large can beef stew   1/4 cup sour cream
        1 small can sliced mushrooms   1 T butter
Salad: 4 stalks celery   12 cherry tomatoes
Bread: 2 French rolls
Dessert: 1 pkg frozen peaches   1 pkg frozen strawberries

1. Set table.
   R E L A X

HERS

9

BEEF HAWAIIAN WITH RICE
PINEAPPLE JUICE
SPICED PEACH HALVES
LIME SHERBET

HIS

1. Preheat oven to 350°.
2. Cut 3/4 lb steak into short thin strips.
3. Melt margarine in medium skillet and saute the strips of steak until lightly browned.
4. Add mushrooms and celery; saute, stirring often, for about 5 minutes.
5. Add sweet and sour sauce. Heat.
6. Serve over rice.
7. Pour pineapple juice and serve.

Appetizer: 2 small cans pineapple juice
Entree: 3/4 lb top round steak
4 sliced mushrooms
2 stalks celery
Rice: 2 servings minute rice
Fruit: 1 small can peach halves
Cinnamon and nutmeg
Dessert: 1 pint lime sherbet

2 T margarine
1 1/2 cups canned sweet and
sour sauce

HERS

1. Set table.
2. Slice the mushrooms and the celery.
3. Open can of peaches, drain, and place in baking dish, cut side up. Sprinkle lightly with cinnamon and nutmeg and place in oven. (They only need to heat, so when beef is ready, remove and serve.)
4. Prepare 2 servings of minute rice.
5. Serve sherbet dessert.

PAM'S LASAGNA
TOSSED GREEN SALAD
GARLIC FRENCH BREAD
LIME JELLO

Entree:	1 1/2 lb ground beef
	1/3 cup sauterne wine
	1 box lasagna noodles
	Parmesan cheese
	1 T cooking oil
	1/2 onion, chopped
	1 small can tomato sauce
	1/2 t brown sugar
	4 slices Mozzarella cheese
Salad:	Greens for salad
	Italian dressing
Bread:	French bread
	Garlic butter
Dessert:	Lime jello (make the night before)

HIS

1. Place large pot half-filled with water over medium heat. Add 1 tsp salt and 1 T cooking oil.
2. Wash and prepare greens for salad.
3. Set table.
4. Melt 1/2 cube of butter over low heat. Mince 1 clove garlice and add to melted butter; stir and turn off heat.
5. Slice loaf of French bread lengthwise; brush each half with melted garlic butter. Brown under broiler for a few minutes. WATCH IT! Don't put the bread in until your partner tells you the lasagna is almost done.
6. Serve French bread cut in 2 - inch slices.
7. Serve dessert.

HERS

1. Preheat oven to 350°.
2. Brown beef in skillet; add onion, salt and pepper. When onion is transparent, drain off grease.
3. Add wine, tomato sauce, and brown sugar. Simmer over low heat for 15 minutes.
4. Add 1/2 package lasagna noodles to the boiling water, stirring occasionally.
5. When noodles are done, drain and rinse with hot tap water.
6. Place layer of noodles in bottom of an 8 X 8 inch baking dish; add a layer of meat sauce and a layer of strips of cheese. Sprinkle with Parmesan cheese. Repeat layers, using rest of ingredients.
7. Place in oven and set timer for 20 minutes.
8. When 5 minutes are left on the timer, add dressing of your choice to salad and toss.
9. Remove lasagna, set oven for broiling temperature (for bread), serve lasagna and salad.

SPEEDY CHOW MEIN WITH CHINESE NOODLES
FRESH ORANGE SLICES
LIME SHERBET WITH FORTUNE COOKIES

HIS

1. Slice celery and chop onion.
2. Peel and section oranges.
3. Set table.
4. Serve sherbet and cookies.

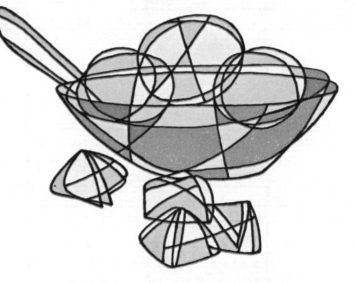

Entree:	2 6-oz "Heat-in-the-pouch" pkgs sirloin tips and gravy
	3/4 cup sliced celery
	1/4 cup chopped onion
	1 8-oz can bean sprouts
	1 1/2 T butter
	3/4 T soy sauce
	1 can Chinese noodles
Fruit:	2 fresh oranges
Dessert:	1 pint lime sherbet
	1 pkg fortune cookies

1. Heat sirloin tips according to package directions.
2. Melt butter in medium-sized skillet; add onion and celery. Saute until they begin to look "clear," then add sirloin tips, bean sprouts and soy sauce.
3. Simmer for 5 minutes and serve over crisp noodles.
4. Serve oranges.

HERS

LIPTON STROGANOFF DINNER
V-8 JUICE
BRUSSEL SPROUTS IN BUTTER SAUCE
BISCUITS
FRESH PINEAPPLE

HIS

1. Preheat oven for biscuits.
2. Set table.
3. Prepare brussel sprouts according to package directions. Check with partner on timing.
4. Bake biscuits according to directions, again checking with partner regarding timing.
5. Serve V-8 juice.
6. Serve brussel sprouts.

18

Appetizer: 2 small cans V-8 juice
Entree: 1 pkg Lipton's Stroganoff Dinner
Bread: 1 pkg refrigerated biscuits
Vegetable: 1 pkg Green Giant brussel sprouts
Dessert: 1 fresh pineapple

1. Prepare stroganoff dinner according to package directions.
2. Peel and core the pineapple, which may then be sliced or cut into chunks, whichever you prefer. Sprinkle with confectioners' sugar and refrigerate until ready to serve dessert.
3. Serve stroganoff and biscuits (don't forget the butter!).
4. Serve dessert.

HERS

BEEF PIES
CITRUS COCKTAIL
TOSSED SALAD
DONUTS

HIS

1. Preheat oven to temperature indicated on beef pie carton.
2. Prepare salad greens: lettuce, chopped celery, sliced radishes, sliced cucumber (don't peel the cucumber, just wash and slice).
3. Place in salad bowl and add "agreed upon" dressing just before serving.
4. Serve donuts.

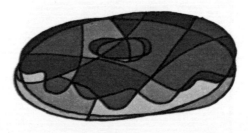
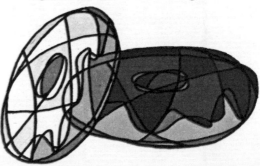

Appetizer:	1 small can grapefruit slices
	1 small can Mandarin oranges
Entree:	2 frozen beef pies
	Dash of paprika
Salad:	Lettuce, celery, cucumber, radishes
	Salad dressing of choice
Dessert:	FRESH bakery donuts

1. Set table.
2. Open cans of fruit, combine contents in bowl and divide into two servings.
3. When oven is ready, sprinkle pies lightly with paprika, place in oven and set timer for specified baking time on package.
4. When timer bell rings, remind partner to add dressing to salad and serve.
5. Remove pies from oven and serve.

HERS

BEEF STEW WITH DUMPLINGS
LETTUCE WITH ROQUEFORT DRESSING
FRESH BERRIES IN SEASON

HIS

1. Open can of beef stew and place in 2-quart saucepan. Add 1/2 cup of water. Place over medium heat and bring to a simmer, stirring occasionally.
2. Prepare lettuce for salad.
3. Set table.
4. When timer rings, add dressing to lettuce and serve.

Entree: 1 large can beef stew
          1 cup prepared biscuit mix
          1/3 cup milk
Salad: Lettuce for two
          Roquefort dressing
Dessert: 2 servings berries

1. Combine biscuit mix with milk and blend gently.
2. When stew is bubbling hot, drop biscuit dough by tablespoonsful onto stew.
   Cover, reduce heat to low, and set timer for 15 minutes.
3. Prepare berries by washing, hulling, or whatever preparation they require, and
   place in dessert dishes. Refrigerate until serving time.
4. Serve stew and dumplings.

HERS

TAHITIAN HAMBURGERS
PINEAPPLE JUICE
HOT GINGER PEARS

Appetizer:	2 small cans pineapple juice
Entree:	1 lb ground round steak
	3/4 t salt
	1 egg
	5 T barbecue sauce
	1/2 cup melted butter
	1 banana
	1 small can pineapple chunks
	4 English muffins
Dessert:	1 small can pears
	1 lemon
	1 T candied ginger
	1 t brown sugar

 **HIS**

1. Preheat broiler
2. Open can of pineapple chunks and drain.
3. Open pear halves.
4. Peel banana and slice diagonally.
5. Cut 3 thick slices of lemon and squeeze 1 T lemon juice from rest of lemon.
6. Combine in saucepan: pear halves and juice, lemon slices, lemon juice, ginger, and brown sugar. Stir and place over very low heat.
7. Allow to simmer for 6 minutes to blend flavors. Turn off heat and cover. The temperature should be just about right by dessert time.
8. Set table. Remember — your partner will need the dinner plates (ovenproof!) for final preparation of the patties under the broiler.
9. Pour pineapple juice — sprinkle lightly with a drop of lemon juice (adds a bit of a tang to "wake up your palate"!).
10. Serve dessert.

HERS

1. Mix steak, salt, and egg thoroughly in bowl. Shape into 4 patties.
2. Place patties on broiler pan and brush with barbecue sauce. Put under broiler.
3. Broil until browned (about 4 minutes), turn and brush other side with barbecue sauce, return to broiler.
4. Split and toast muffins.
5. Place broiled patties on muffin halves.
6. Melt butter in small pan, dip sliced bananas in the melted butter and arrange slices around patties on each plate.
7. Dip pineapple chunks in barbecue sauce and place on banana slices. Slide back in broiler to heat fruit — about 2 minutes. Be sure your plates are ovenproof! (Extra muffin halves can be served on an extra plate or in a bread basket.)
8. Serve patties and fruit.

MARIE'S BEEF AND RICE
RELISHES: CARROT AND CELERY STICKS,
OLIVES, CHERRY TOMATOES
SLICED STRAWBERRIES WITH CREAM

HIS

1. Chop onion.
2. Cut peppers in half, remove seeds, and cut into small squares.
3. Prepare relishes: carrot sticks, celery sticks, olives, and cherry tomatoes.
4. Hull and slice strawberries.
5. Serve dessert.

Entree:	1 lb ground beef	1 8-oz can tomato sauce
	2 cups minute rice	Salt and pepper to taste
	1/2 onion	1 T milk
	2 bell peppers	
Relishes:	1 carrot	
	2 stalks celery	
	10 cherry tomatoes	
	Ripe olives	
Dessert:	1 pint fresh strawberries	1/2 pint cream

1. Preheat oven to 325°.
2. Brown beef in skillet, adding onion and peppers when pink color has **HERS** disappeared. Simmer until peppers are tender; season to taste.
3. Prepare minute rice and add to beef mixture along with 1 T milk. Mix thoroughly.
4. Place this mixture in a baking dish. Combine tomato sauce and 1/2 tomato sauce can of water in a bowl and pour over top of mixture.
5. Place in oven for 20 minutes (set timer) and serve from the baking dish.
6. Set table.

MEAT LOAF
BEEF RICE-A-RONI
FRENCH-CUT GREEN BEANS WITH ALMONDS
CINNAMON ROLLS

1. Preheat oven to 325°.
2. Set table.
3. When about 25 minutes remain on timer, begin preparing Rice-a-roni according to package directions.
4. When meat loaf is removed from oven, turn oven off and place cinnamon rolls on a piece of foil large enough to cover completely, and place in the oven. They should be hot and fresh when you are ready for dessert.
5. Serve Rice-a-roni.

30

Entree:	1 lb ground beef
	1 small can tomato sauce
	1 T instant minced onion
	1 t dried parsley flakes
	2 eggs
	Salt and pepper to season
	2 slices bacon
Vegetable:	1 pkg Green Giant french-cut green beans with almonds
Rice:	1 pkg beef Rice-a-roni
Dessert:	2 cinnamon rolls (bakery fresh, if possible!)

1. Combine beef, tomato sauce, onion, parsley, eggs, salt and pepper in bowl and mix thoroughly.
2. Shape the mixture into a loaf in an oblong baking pan. Top with strips of bacon and place in the oven. Set timer for 40 minutes.
3. When partner has covered the Rice-a-roni to let it simmer, start preparing the beans according to package instructions.
4. Serve meat loaf and beans.

HERS

SLOPPY JOES
CREAM OF CELERY SOUP
VANILLA ICE CREAM WITH SLICED STRAWBERRIES

HIS

1. Open soup, place in pan, and gradually add milk, stirring constantly until thoroughly mixed. Place over low heat.
2. Preheat oven to 300º.
3. Set table.
4. Hull and slice strawberries and refrigerate until dessert-serving time.
5. When Sloppy Joe sauce is almost ready, place buns on cookie sheet and put in the oven to warm.
6. Serve soup in cups or bowls. Garnish with chopped parsley, finely chopped celery, or freshly ground pepper.

32

Soup:	1 can cream of celery soup	1 soup can milk or half-and-half
Entree:	2 hamburger buns	
	3/4 lb ground beef	
	1 jar Ragu spaghetti sauce with mushrooms	
	1/2 onion	
	1 t Worchestershire sauce	
	1/2 T brown sugar	
Dessert:	1 pint vanilla ice cream	
	A few choice strawberries	

1. Chop onion.
2. Put beef into a medium-size skillet, season with salt and pepper and cook until beef is lightly browned or no pink color is showing.
3. Push hamburger to one side of skillet and add onion, sauteing lightly. Mix beef and onions, and drain off excess drippings.
4. Add Ragu sauce, Worchestershire sauce, and brown sugar. Mix well.
5. Turn heat to low and simmer for about 10 minutes, stirring often.
6. Serve on buns. (These are rightly named, so have napkins handy and don't use your best white tablecloth!)

HERS

**KIP'S GROUND BEEF CURRY
RICE
CONDIMENTS
DATE CAKES**

HIS

1. Chop onion.
2. Put olive oil in medium skillet and saute onion until golden.
3. Push onion to side of pan and drop meat by teaspoonsful into the pan; add salt and brown on all sides. Add curry powder and saute for about 1 minute.
4. Blend 2 T of bouillon with the cornstarch to make a paste; pour remaining bouillon into pan and bring to a boil. Stir in paste and cook, stirring gently, until thickened. Add lemon juice and blend.
5. Turn curried meat into a hot serving bowl and serve.
6. Serve dessert.

34

Entree:	1 small onion	1 t curry powder
	1 t olive oil	1 cup beef bouillon
	1 lb ground round steak	1 t cornstarch
	1/2 t salt	1 t lemon juice
Rice:	1 1/4 cups minute rice	
Condiments:	1/4 cup flaked coconut	
	1/2 cup chopped cashews	
	1/2 cucumber, chopped	
	1 small can pineapple tidbits, drained	
Dessert:	Date cakes purchased at your local bakery	

1. Prepare rice according to package directions.
2. Place condiments in small individual bowls.
3. Set table.
4. Serve rice and condiments.

HERS

MARINATED LAMB CHOPS
SLICED TOMATOES WITH FRENCH DRESSING
HASH-BROWN POTATOES WITH GREEN ONIONS
NECTARINE SLICES IN SOUR CREAM

Entree: 2 shoulder lamb chops
             2 T brown sugar
             4 T soy sauce
Potatoes: 1 pkg frozen hash-brown potatoes
             2 green onions
Salad: 2 tomatoes
             2 lettuce leaves
             French dressing
Dessert: 2 nectarines
             1/2 cup sour cream
             2 T brown sugar

 **HIS**

Lemon Marinade:

Combine and mix: 1 cup lemon juice, 3/4 cup corn oil, 1 chopped medium onion, 1 clove crushed garlic, 1 t powdered thyme, 2 crushed bay leaves, and 1 T freshly ground pepper.

1. Chops MUST be placed in marinade the night before.
2. Set table.
3. Slice green onions — including part of tops.
4. Slice tomatoes and arrange on lettuce leaves.
5. Prepare nectarine slices, place in bowl, add sour cream and brown sugar. Stir together gently.
6. Spoon into dessert dishes and refrigerate. (Top with chopped nuts if desired.)
7. Help your partner with the potatoes — watching the chops can be a full-time task and turning the potatoes will be a help.
8. Serve tomato slices and potatoes.

HERS

1. Preheat oven to broiling temperature.
2. Remove chops from marinade and place under broiler.
3. Put 1/4 cup cooking oil in skillet, heat, and add potatoes and onions.
4. Turn chops from time to time. When nicely browned, season to taste and serve.
5. Stir and turn the potatoes and onions frequently so they get crispy and golden brown. Partner will help with these.
6. Place French dressing in small bowl and set on table.
7. Serve dessert.

BROILED PORK CHOPS
APPLESAUCE
CORN ON THE COB
BREAD STICKS
CANTALOUPE

HIS

1. Preheat broiler.
2. Trim pork chops. Make small cuts in top edge of each chop to prevent curling.
3. Dot chops with butter and place under broiler, checking often, and brown on both sides.
4. While chops are browning, open bread sticks and place them in a large decorative mug or bread basket.
5. Prepare cantaloupe by cutting in half and scooping out the seeds.
6. Serve chops.
7. Serve cantaloupe for dessert.

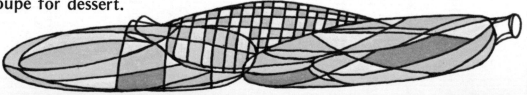

Entree:	4 medium pork chops
	Butter
	1 jar applesauce
Vegetable:	4 ears fresh corn
	Butter and salt
Bread:	1 pkg bread sticks
Dessert:	1 cantaloupe

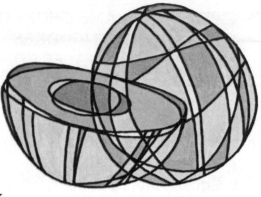

HERS

1. Heat water in large pan, adding 1 T salt.
2. Husk and wash corn, removing all the silk.
3. Set table.
4. When water is boiling, add the corn, bring to a rapid boil again, cover, and turn off the heat. Set your timer for 10 minutes. DO NOT UNCOVER PAN UNTIL THE TIMER RINGS.
5. While waiting for water to boil for the corn, place applesauce in a pan over low heat, adding 1 T powdered sugar and 1/2 t nutmeg (preferably freshly ground!).
6. Serve corn and applesauce.

LAMB CHOPS ITALIANO
ARTICHOKES
NOODLES ROMANOFF
SPUMONE ICE CREAM

HIS

1. Fill 3-quart saucepan half full of water and add 2 t salt. Bring to rapid boil.
2. Wash artichokes and trim stems if too long. When water boils, cook artichokes over medium heat for 45 minutes. Set timer.
3. Prepare Noodles Romanoff according to package directions, calculating time so noodles are ready when artichokes are cooked.
4. Melt butter for artichokes and add lemon juice just before serving.
5. Serve artichokes and noodles.

Entree:	2 lamb chops, 1-inch thick	1/4 t oregano
	Salt and pepper	2 slices tomato
	1/4 t garlic salt	2 slices Mozzarella cheese
Vegetable:	2 fresh artichokes	
	Butter	
Noodles:	1 pkg Noodles Romanoff	
Dessert:	1 pint Spumone ice cream	

HERS

1. Set table.
2. Combine garlic salt, oregano, salt and pepper.
3. Preheat broiler.
4. Slice tomato (2 slices only), and remove 2 slices Mozzarella cheese from package.
5. Sprinkle half of seasoning mixture over chops and place them under broiler for 10 minutes.
6. Turn chops, sprinkle with rest of seasoning, and broil for another 8 minutes.
7. Place 1 slice tomato and 1 slice of cheese on each chop. Return to broiler until cheese melts and is lightly brown. Serve.
8. Serve dessert.

LAMB CHOPS CALIFORNIA
BABY PEAS IN BUTTER SAUCE
NOODLES PARMESAN
BUFFET RYE BREAD
LIME JELLO WITH WHIPPED CREAM TOPPING

Entree:	3 lamb chops (shoulder or loin)
	1/4 t garlic salt
	Freshly ground pepper
	3 slices fresh tomato
	1/3 cup white chablis wine
	1/2 t finely chopped parsley
Noodles:	1 pkg Noodles Parmesan
Vegetables:	1 pkg Green Giant baby peas in butter sauce
Bread:	1 loaf buffet rye bread
Dessert:	1 pkg lime jello (made the night before)
	1/2 pint whipping cream or commercial topping

45

 **HIS**

1. Set table.
2. Cook peas according to package directions.
3. Cook noodles according to package directions.
4. Pour a glass of chablis for each of you — if desired.
5. When timer rings for chops, serve peas and noodles Parmesan.
6. Serve dessert.

OHERS

1. Trim excess fat from chops and brown them quickly in a hot skillet with just a trace of cooking oil — or use the trimmings to coat the pan, remove them, and add the chops.
2. Sprinkle salt and freshly ground pepper over chops; top each chop with a tomato slice.
3. Pour the wine over all, cover pan tightly, and turn heat to simmer. Set timer for 20 minutes.
4. If you wish, you may thicken the pan juices slightly with a little cornstarch mixed with cold water. They are very good au naturel, however.
5. Whip the cream, adding 2 t sugar and 1/2 t vanilla. Refrigerate until dessert time.
6. Serve chops and rye bread.

BROILED HAM STEAK
YAMS
FRESH PINEAPPLE
CHOCOLATE PUDDING

HIS

1. Prepare pudding according to package directions. Refrigerate.
2. Prepare pineapple and cut into bite-size pieces. Sprinkle with confectioners' sugar, stir lightly, and refrigerate.
3. Set table.
4. Serve pineapple when ham and yams are ready.
5. Serve dessert.

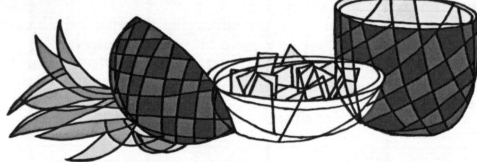

48

Entree: 2 slices cooked ham (1/2 − 1 inch thick)
Potatoes: 1 small can yams
Fruit: 1 fresh pineapple
Dessert: 1 pkg instant chocolate pudding

HERS

1. Preheat broiler.
2. Place yams and liquid in a small pan over low heat.
3. Place ham slices under broiler, turning when lightly browned. (The ham is already cooked, you are only heating it thoroughly and making it look more attractive.)
4. Drain yams, place in serving dish, put about 1 T of butter on top and sprinkle lightly with freshly ground nutmeg.
5. Serve yams with ham steaks.

RALPH'S BRAISED VEAL CHOPS
TOMATO JUICE COCKTAIL
NOODLES PARMESAN
FRENCH-CUT GREEN BEANS
CHOCOLATE CAKE

HIS

1. Remove cake from freezer and set table.
2. Prepare noodles according to directions on package.
3. Cook beans according to directions. Enhance beans with 1/2 t of fresh lemon juice.
4. While the above items are cooking, pour the tomato juice and add a dash of Tabasco sauce.

REMEMBER:
It will take your partner about 50 minutes to prepare the chops, so plan your activities accordingly. (A small glass of wine or a well prepared martini might be a nice contribution to the congenial kitchen atmosphere.)

50

Appetizer:	2 small cans tomato juice	
	Dash of Tabasco sauce	
Entree:	4 veal chops	1 cup bouillon
	4 T butter	1/2 cup sour cream
	1 T chopped onion	
Noodles:	1 pkg Noodles Parmesan	Butter and seasonings
Vegetable:	1 pkg french-cut green beans	
Dessert:	1 Pepperidge Farms frozen chocolate cake	

HERS

1. Melt butter in skillet, add chopped onion and saute until soft. Remove.
2. Dredge chops in flour, sprinkle with salt freshly ground pepper, and brown in skillet.
3. Add bouillon cube to 1 cup hot water; dissolve, stir, and pour over chops. Put sauteed onions on top of the chops (adding more water if necessary to bring depth to about 1/4 inch).
4. Cover and simmer for 30 minutes. Add sour cream and let stand for a few minutes until cream is hot, <u>not</u> simmering, and serve.

SPARERIBS
SLICED TOMATOES
CORN ON THE COB
SLICED PEACHES

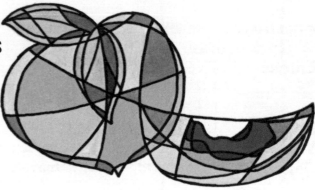

HIS

1. Preheat oven to 350°.
2. Wipe ribs with a damp cloth and sprinkle generously on both sides with Lawry's Seasoned Salt.
3. Place on rack over broiler pan and place in oven. Set timer for 1 hour.
4. Peel and slice peaches and place in dessert dishes. Sprinkle lightly with lemon juice.
5. Sprinkle brown sugar over peaches and refrigerate.
6. When ribs are done, cut apart and serve. Don't forget the napkins!
7. Serve dessert.

Entree:	1 1/2 lbs spareribs
	Lawry's Seasoned Salt
Vegetables:	2 fresh tomatoes
	4 ears of fresh corn
	Butter, salt and pepper
Dessert:	2 fresh peaches
	1 t fresh lemon juice
	1 T brown sugar

HERS

1. Set table.
2. Husk corn, removing all the silk.
3. When about 20 minutes remain on the timer, half fill a 3-quart pan with water, add 1 T salt and bring to a full boil.
4. When water is boiling, add corn, bring to a full boil again, cover and turn off heat. DO NOT REMOVE COVER FOR 10 MINUTES.
5. Slice tomatoes and refrigerate.
6. When ribs are done, serve corn and tomatoes.

LIVER A LA BURGUNDY
SLICED TOMATOES
MASHED POTATOES
ICE CREAM

HIS

1. Make sauce for liver as follows. Combine onion, mushrooms, wine, and garlic salt. Place over low heat, stirring occasionally until heated. Remove from stove and inform partner that sauce is ready when needed.
2. Assemble ingredients for potatoes. Preparation time is just a few minutes, so ask your partner to let you know when liver is almost ready to serve, then prepare potatoes.
3. Set table.
4. Serve potatoes.
5. Serve dessert.

54

Entree:	1 lb calves liver	Flour, garlic salt,
	1 small can button mushrooms	freshly ground pepper
	1 medium-size onion	1/2 cube butter or margarine
	1/3 cup burgundy wine	
Potatoes:	2 cups instant mashed potatoes	
Vegetable:	2 tomatoes	
Dessert:	Your favorite ice cream	

1. Prepare a mixture of flour, salt, and pepper. Dredge liver in mixture.
2. Melt butter. Place liver in pan and brown on both sides.
3. Pour sauce partner has prepared over liver, lifting each piece slightly so sauce can flow under and around it, and simmer over very low heat for 20 minutes. Set timer.
4. Slice tomatoes and arrange on serving plate.
5. Serve liver in shallow dish, topped with sauce.

HERS

EASY BAKED CHICKEN WITH SPICED CRABAPPLES
MIXED VEGETABLES
RYE TOAST
CHOCOLATE PUDDING

HIS

1. Set table.
2. When about 20 minutes remain on the timer for the chicken, prepare vegetables according to package directions.
3. Make toast just before timer will ring to signal the end of baking time for the chicken.
4. Open jar of spiced apples and place in serving dish.
5. Serve dessert (When and if either of you should <u>want</u> any dessert!)

56

Entree:	1 broiling chicken, split in two Salt and freshly ground pepper
	4 T butter or margarine
Condiments:	1 small jar spiced crabapples
Vegetable:	1 pkg Green Giant mixed vegetables with butter sauce
Bread:	Rye bread for toast
Dessert:	1 container Cool & Creamy chocolate pudding

1. Preheat oven to 450⁰.
2. Spread a thick coat of margarine on the inside of a 3-quart casserole.
3. Place chicken halves in casserole, skin side up.
4. Sprinkle with salt and pepper and dot with remaining margarine.
5. Cover with a tight-fitting lid and place in preheated oven, setting timer for 30–35 minutes. DO NOT PEEK DURING BAKING TIME!
6. Serve directly from casserole.

HERS

CHICKEN BREASTS WITH RICE
APPLE JUICE
LIMA BEANS IN BUTTER SAUCE
ORANGE SLICES WITH VIENNA FINGERS

HIS

1. Set table.
2. Quarter onion.
3. When timer shows 20 minutes remaining, prepare lima beans according to package directions.
4. Remove rind from oranges and slice.
5. Arrange orange slices on dessert plates, placing two cookies on each plate. Refrigerate until ready to serve.
6. Serve lima beans and apple juice.

Appetizer:	2 small cans apple juice	1/4 cup dry white wine
Entree:	2 chicken breasts	1/4 cup tomato soup
	Flour	1/4 cup cold water
	1 clove garlic	1/4 cup raw rice
	1 onion	
Vegetable:	1 pkg Green Giant lima beans with butter sauce	
Dessert:	2 fresh oranges	1 pkg Vienna fingers

HERS

1. Melt butter in heavy skillet, add garlic clove.
2. Add onion and saute until transparent. Remove garlic clove.
3. Salt and pepper chicken breasts and dust with flour. Place in skillet and brown on both sides.
4. Pour white wine over chicken; remove chicken to a plate.
5. Add rice to skillet and saute 2 minutes. Mix soup and water; stir into rice.
6. Place chicken on rice and spoon some of the liquid over the chicken. Turn heat to low, cover, and simmer for 30 minutes. Set timer. Stir occasionally, adding water if necessary.
7. Serve by again removing chicken to plate, put the rice into a shallow serving dish and place the chicken on top of the rice.

CHICKEN POT PIE
PEAS IN BUTTER SAUCE
BROILED GRAPEFRUIT

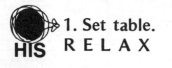

HIS 1. Set table.
R E L A X

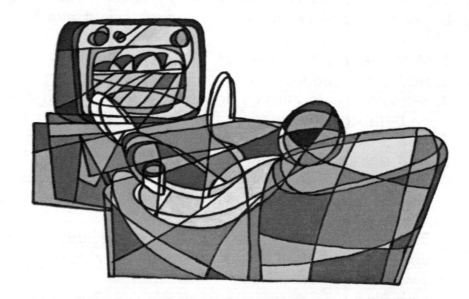

60

Entree: 2 frozen chicken pot pies
Vegetable: 1 pkg Green Giant peas in butter sauce
Dessert: 1 large grapefruit
            1 T butter
            Cinnamon-sugar mixture

1. Preheat oven to prescribed temperature for pot pies.
2. When oven is ready, place pies in oven and set timer.
3. Cook peas according to package directions, planning time for pies to bake and peas to be done at the same time.
4. Halve grapefruit; cut around sections for easy eating, and cut out the center.
5. Fill center hole in grapefruit with butter and sprinkle with mixture of cinnamon and sugar (1 part cinnamon to 4 parts sugar). Place in shallow baking dish.
6. When pies are done, remove them from the oven and turn on the broiler, placing the grapefruit about 4 inches below heat. When they are lightly brown and bubbling on top, remove. Serve for dessert.
7. Serve pies and peas.
8. Rouse relaxed partner and inform same that dinner is served.

CORNISH HEN
ENDIVE SALAD
CHICKEN RICE-A-RONI
RED APPLE SLICES AND GOUDA CHEESE

HIS

1. Set table.
2. Wash endive and break into bite-size pieces. Place in salad bowls. Refrigerate until ready to serve.
3. When about 20 minutes remain on the timer for Cornish hen, prepare Rice-a-roni according to directions.
4. Add olive oil to endive, toss well; add vinegar and toss well. Sprinkle lightly with salt and freshly ground pepper.
5. Serve Rice-a-roni.

Entree:	1 Cornish hen	1/2 cup honey
	1 cup soy sauce	2 large cloves garlic, crushed
Salad:	1 endive	
	2 T olive oil	
	1 T vinegar	
	Salt and pepper	
Rice:	1 pkg Chicken Rice-a-roni	
Dessert:	2 red apples	
	1 small Gouda cheese	

1. Preheat oven to 375°.
2. Wash and dry Cornish hen. Season inside and out with salt and pepper; place in baking pan.
3. Combine soy sauce, honey, and garlic; brush mixture over Cornish hen.
4. Place in oven and set timer for 45 minutes. Baste occasionally with soy-honey mixture.
5. Slice apples and cut wedges of cheese. Arrange on dessert plate and refrigerate.
6. Serve Cornish hen.
7. Serve dessert.

CHICKEN LIVERS WITH MUSHROOMS
CHEESE AND PEAR SALAD
LEMON PUDDING

HIS

1. Set table.
2. Open pears and mix 2 T pear juice with cream cheese. Fill pear halves with mixture and press halves together.
3. Place lettuce leaf on each salad plate, put whole pear on lettuce leaf, and top with mayonnaise. Add a dash of nutmeg to top of each salad.
4. When chicken livers are almost done, make toast.
5. Serve dessert.

64

Entree:	2 slices bacon	Dash of pepper
	6 chicken livers	1 t flour
	6 mushrooms	1/4 cup cream
	1/2 t salt	2 slices toast
Salad:	2 T pear juice	
	4 pear halves	
	1 1/2 oz cream cheese (1/2 pkg)	
	2 lettuce leaves	
	1/4 cup mayonnaise	
	Dash of nutmeg	
Dessert:	1 pkg Instant Lemon Pudding	

1. Make pudding according to package directions. Refrigerate.
2. Dice bacon, livers, and mushrooms.
3. Saute bacon until almost crisp, add livers, mushrooms, salt and pepper.
4. Saute for about 5 minutes, stirring occasionally — very gently.
5. In a separate saucepan, make a sauce of flour and cream; add to livers.
6. Serve on toast
7. Serve salads.

HERS

LOBSTER-AVOCADO SALAD
CREAM OF MUSHROOM SOUP
BAKE AND SERVE ROLLS
FRUIT TARTS

HIS

1. Set oven temperature for rolls.
2. Prepare 1 can soup, using milk.
3. Place pan containing soup over low heat, stirring often. **DO NOT BOIL.**
4. Place rolls in oven, setting timer for specified time on package.
5. Remove fruit tarts from freezer and place on baking sheet.
6. When rolls are baked, remove them, adjust oven temperature for tarts, and put tarts in oven to bake. Set timer.
7. Pour soup into mugs or bowls and serve.
8. When timer rings, remove tarts from oven and sprinkle with confectioners' sugar. Transfer to dessert plates to cool.

Soup:	1 can Cream of Mushroom soup
	1 soup-can of milk
Entree:	1 avocado
	3/4 cup lobster
	2 lettuce leaves
	Russian dressing
	Cherry tomatoes or olives for garnish
Bread:	2-4 Bake 'n Serve rolls
Dessert:	2 frozen fruit tarts

1. Set table.
2. Place large lettuce leaf on each salad plate.
3. Peel and halve avocado. Remove seed and place one half on each lettuce leaf.
4. Combine 3/4 cup lobster with enough Russian dressing to blend.
5. Fill avocado halves with lobster mixture and garnish with olives or cherry tomatoes. Serve.
6. If your partner has been too busy with the tarts, place the rolls in a bread basket and cover with a napkin to preserve their warmth.

HERS

PERCH IN FOIL
FRUIT SALAD WALDORF
BAKE AND SERVE ROLLS
ICE CREAM WITH CREME DE MENTHE

Entree: 4 perch (1 1/2 lb)
            Foil
            3 T butter
            1 bay leaf
            1/8 t salt
            1 T lemon juice
            2 T flour

Salad: 1 orange
            1 small can pineapple chunks
            12 miniature marshmallows
            1/3 cup sour cream

Bread: 4 Bake 'n Serve rolls

Dessert: 1 pint vanilla ice cream
            2 oz creme de menthe

 HIS

1. Set table.
2. Place all of the following items in a 1 quart bowl: 1 orange, rind removed and slices cut into bite sized pieces; 4 - 5 walnut halves, coarsely chopped; 1 small can pineapple chunks, drained; 1 dozen miniature marshmallows; enough sour cream to coat ingredients, about 1/3 cup.
3. Mix gently.
4. Prepare 1 small box Jello according to package directions. Pour into 4 dessert dishes or parfait glasses. Refrigerate for tomorrow night's dessert - or if you prefer, a low calorie late-night snack.
5. Serve salad.

HERS

1. Preheat oven to 400⁰.
2. Tear pieces of foil large enough to wrap each perch.
3. Put 3 T butter or margarine into a small skillet over low heat. Add 1 small bay leaf, 1/8 tsp garlic powder, 1/8 tsp salt and 1 T lemon juice. Stir until butter is melted and the ingredients are well blended. Remove from heat.
4. Lightly flour the perch, place them on their separate pieces of foil and pour about 1/2 (or divide evenly if you have more than 2 perch!) of the butter mixture over each fish. Sprinkle with freshly ground pepper, wrap foil around fish and place in oven.
5. Set timer for 15 - 20 minutes.
6. Bake rolls according to package directions, timing their placement in the oven so they may be removed at the same time as the perch.
7. Serve perch and rolls.

71

SAUTEED OYSTERS PATRICIAN
FRESH PEAR HALVES
LIME SHERBET AND OREO COOKIES

HIS

1. Finely crush (try a rolling pin) 12 soda crackers.
2. Prepare pear halves.
3. Prepare lemon wedges.
4. Set table.
5. Make toast when oysters are almost done.
6. Serve dessert.

Entree: 10 fresh oysters
4 T butter
1/2 cup cracker crumbs

1 T sherry
1 lemon
2 slices toast

Fruit: 2 fresh pears
Dessert: 1 pint lime sherbet

Oreo Cookies

HERS

1. Rinse oysters; drain on paper towels to remove excess moisture.
2. Melt butter in skillet using low heat.
3. Dip the oysters in the melted butter, then in cracker crumbs, then return to skillet. Saute, turning when lightly browned. This takes about 10 minutes.
4. Place oysters on toast, sprinkle with sherry, and serve with lemon wedges.

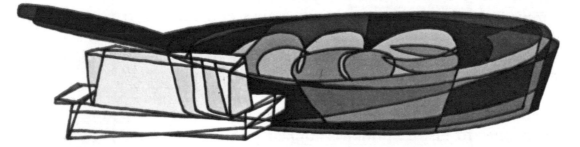

73

SALMON STEAKS
DELICATESSEN COLESLAW
BUTTERED NOODLES
CANTALOUPE WITH SUGARED GRAPES

HIS

1. Fill a 3-quart saucepan 1/2 full of water for cooking noodles, adding 1 T cooking oil and 1 t salt. Set over medium heat.
2. While waiting for water to boil, wash grapes and remove from stems. Drain on paper towel, place on a shallow plate and sprinkle with sugar.
3. Add noodles to boiling water, cook according to package directions or until tender.
4. Prepare cantaloupe. Refrigerate.
5. Drain noodles when tender, place in serving bowl. Add 1 generous T of butter, salt and pepper to taste. Sprinkle chopped parsley over top for garnish. Serve.

74

Entree:	2 salmon steaks	Salt and freshly ground pepper
	1 clove garlic	1 T fresh parsley
	2 T butter	
Noodles:	Noodles for 2 (about 2 cups dry)	
	1 T butter	Salt and pepper
Salad:	1 pint coleslaw	
Dessert:	1 small cantaloupe	
	1 medium-size bunch seedless grapes	
	1 T sugar	

1. Melt butter with garlic clove in skillet, add salmon steaks, and brown on both sides; season with salt and freshly ground pepper.
2. Cover and let simmer over very low heat about 10 minutes, turning 2 or 3 times.
3. Set table.
4. Chop a small amount of parsley for garnish with noodles.
5. Open coleslaw and place in serving dish.
6. Serve steaks and coleslaw.

HERS

KOLL'S SALMON KASSEROLE
PEAS WITH MUSHROOMS AND ONIONS
CHOCOLATE MINT COOKIES

HIS

1. Prepare 3 cups instant mashed potatoes.
2. Wash and peel onion; wash mushrooms.
3. Cut both onion and mushrooms into small pieces.
4. In a heavy skillet, heat 3 T cooking oil, add onion and mushrooms. Saute until onions are semi-transparent.
5. Add peas and saute, stirring often, about 5 minutes over medium heat.
6. Reduce heat to low, cover, and leave over heat for another 3 minutes. Season with salt, pepper, and garlic salt. Serve.

76

Entree:	1 large can red salmon	2 cups instant mashed potatoes
	1 can mushroom soup	
Vegetable:	1/2 cup frozen peas	Salt, pepper, garlic salt
	4 fresh mushrooms	3 T cooking oil
	1 onion	
Dessert:	1 pkg chocolate mint cookies	

1. Preheat broiler.
2. Combine salmon and mushroom soup in a saucepan and heat.
3. Set table.
4. Place hot mixture in buttered casserole.
5. Spread mashed potatoes over mixture to form a layer.
6. Sprinkle with paprika and brown under broiler.
7. Serve directly from casserole.

HERS

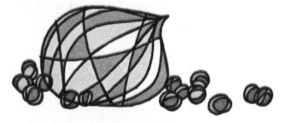

NANCY'S EMERGENCY SPAGHETTI WITH TUNA SAUCE
TOSSED GREEN SALAD
LEMON PUDDING AND PEANUT BUTTER COOKIES

HIS

1. Chop onion and garlic clove. (Hint: A garlic press is a handy asset to any kitchen — you'll use it more often than you might think.)
2. Prepare enough spaghetti for two servings. Remember, it "grows" during cooking. A teaspoon of cooking oil in the water prevents it from sticking together.
3. Wash and prepare salad greens.
4. Drain spaghetti in colander. Add 2 inches of hot water to spaghetti pan and set the colander in the pan. This will keep the spaghetti hot and moist for any second helpings.
5. Place peanut butter cookies on serving plate when you are both ready for dessert.

Entree:	2 small can tuna	1 small onion
	1 pkg spaghetti	Dash of basil
	1 can tomato paste	1 clove of garlic, minced
	1/2 tomato paste can of dry vermouth	1 T olive oil
Salad:	Greens — your choice	
	Your favorite dressing	
Dessert:	1 pkg instant butterscotch pudding	

HERS

1. Set table.
2. Heat a small amount of olive oil in a medium-size skillet; add onion, garlic, and saute until soft.
3. Add tuna, tomato paste, and vermouth; sprinkle with basil. Add salt and freshly ground pepper to taste.
4. Cover and let simmer over very low heat for 8 minutes.
5. Add dressing to salad greens your partner has prepared, and serve.
6. While sauce is simmering, prepare pudding according to package directions and place in serving dishes. Refrigerate until you wish to serve.
7. Serve sauce over spaghetti.

ERIC'S TUNA SKILLET DINNER
WHOLE WHEAT ROLLS
BERRIES IN CUSTARD SAUCE

HIS

1. Coarsely chop onion and saute in 1 T butter until transparent.
2. Add soup, milk and peas. Cover and heat just to boiling point, stirring occasionally.
3. Add tuna and dash of pepper; heat, but do not boil.
4. Serve over chow mein noodles.
5. Serve dessert.

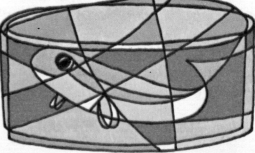

Entree:	1/2 medium onion	1/2 cup frozen peas
	1 T butter	1 6-1/2 oz can tuna
	1 can frozen condensed cream of shrimp soup	Dash of pepper
	1 small can chow mein noodles	1/3 cup milk
Rolls:	4 whole wheat Bake 'n Serve rolls	
Dessert:	1 pkg instant vanilla pudding	
	1/2 t vanilla	
	1/2 pint fresh strawberries	

1. Preheat oven to temperature required for rolls; bake according to directions.
2. Hull, wash and slice strawberries, reserving 4 for dessert topping.
3. Make pudding according to package instructions.
4. Divide sliced berries into dessert dishes, pour pudding over the berries and top with whole berries. Refrigerate.
5. Put chow mein noodles in shallow baking dish and place in oven for a few minutes to crisp.
6. Set table.
7. Serve rolls; put chow mein noodles in serving dish.

HERS

JAN'S TUNA CASSEROLE
FRESH PEACH HALVES
RYE TOAST
RAISIN-SPICE COOKIES

HIS

1. Put 2 eggs in salted water to boil. Use low heat. When water bubbles gently, set timer for 10 minutes.
2. Preheat oven to 350°.
3. Halve peaches, remove pit, and peel.
4. Peel and chop eggs when done.
5. When timer is about to ring for casserole, toast and butter rye bread.
6. Prepare cookies for baking on cookie sheet according to package directions.
7. When casserole is removed from oven, adjust oven temperature if necessary and place cookies in oven. Set timer.

Entree: 1/3 cup milk   1 cup cooked peas or mixed vegetables
         1 7-oz can tuna   1 can mushroom soup
         2 hard-boiled eggs   1 cup crumbled potato chips
Fruit: 2 fresh peaches
Bread: Rye toast
         butter
Dessert: 1 pkg ready-to-bake raisin spice cookies

1. Check refrigerator for any leftover vegetables. If the results are negative, put
   water in pan and cook 1 cup peas or mixed vegetables.
2. Open tuna, drain, and flake.
3. Crumble potato chips.
4. Blend soup and milk in a 1-quart casserole.
5. Stir in tuna, eggs, and peas. Top with chips and place in oven, setting timer for
   25-30 minutes.
6. Set table.
7. If you make a great martini - - now would be a nice time to do your thing.
8. Don't forget the cookies!

HERS

PLANKED FISH FILLETS
CARROTS AND BROCCOLI
MASHED POTATOES
BALI HAI DELIGHT

Entree: 1 lb fish fillets, fresh or frozen   1/2 t salt
1 T cooking oil   1/4 t paprika
1 T lemon juice   Freshly ground pepper

Potatoes: 2 cups instant mashed potatoes
Butter, salt, and pepper to taste

Vegetable: 1 cup frozen carrots
1 pkg frozen broccoli

Dessert: 4 chopped walnut meats
10 miniature marshmallows
3/4 cup sour cream
1 small can pineapple chunks and juice
1 small can mandarin oranges, drained

If fish are frozen, thaw at least partially before cooking.

HIS

1. Preheat oven to 350⁰.
2. Rinse fish with cold water, pat dry with paper towel.
3. Place in single layer, skin side down on oiled plank - or well-greased bake-and-serve platter.
4. Combine cooking oil, lemon juice, salt, paprika, and a dash of freshly ground pepper in measuring cup.
5. Pour mixture over fish and place in oven. Set timer for 20 minutes. Test for doneness. Fish flakes easily with a fork when done, so leave it in for an additional 5 minutes or so if you think it needs more cooking.
6. Prepare mashed potatoes (instant variety!).
7. Remove fish from oven and assist partner in arranging vegetables around entree.

HERS

1. Set table.
2. Prepare carrots and broccoli according to package directions. Begin when timer is set for baking the fish.
3. Open oranges, drain; open pineapple chunks. Place both in medium-sized bowl.
4. Chop walnuts and add to bowl, along with marshmallows and sour cream. Mix gently, put into serving dishes, and refrigerate.
5. When fish is done and removed from oven, arrange drained, seasoned vegetables around fish on serving platter or plank. Mashed potatoes can also be placed in mounds on the same platter, alternating with the vegetables for a very colorful and appetizing effect. (A dash of paprika on the potatoes, please!)
6. Serve dessert.

CRAB NEWBURG
PINEAPPLE AND STRAWBERRY SALAD PLATE
GINGERBREAD

HIS

1. Remove shell or cartilage from crab meat. Melt butter in skillet over low heat and blend in flour and seasonings.
2. Add cream gradually and cook until thick and smooth, stirring constantly.
3. Stir a little of the sauce into the egg yolks, then add to skillet. Keep stirring!
4. Add crab meat and heat — do not boil.
5. Remove from heat and stir in sherry.
6. Serve on toast points.

Entree:	1/2 lb crab meat	3/4 cup heavy cream
	3 T butter	2 egg yolks, beaten
	1 1/2 T flour	1 T sherry
	1/4 t salt	Toast points
	1/4 t paprika	
Salad:	1 cup pineapple chunks	
	1 cup fresh strawberries	
Dessert:	1 pkg gingerbread mix	

HERS

1. Preheat oven and prepare gingerbread according to package directions. Set timer.
2. Set table.
3. Open pineapple, drain; hull and slice berries.
4. Combine pineapple and berries in bowl, mix gently and serve.
5. Make toast points.
6. Serve gingerbread while still warm.

CRAB LOUIS
FRESH FRENCH BREAD
LEMON PUDDING

HIS

1. Boil two eggs gently for 10 minutes. (Do this the night before if possible.)
2. Preheat oven to 250°.
3. Make lemon pudding according to package directions and refrigerate.
4. Wrap French bread in foil and place in oven.
5. Slice cucumber and tomatoes.
6. When eggs are done, drain off water and run cold water over them; remove shells and slice.
7. When salad is ready to serve, remove bread from oven, slice, and serve with lots of butter.
8. Serve dessert when ready.

90

Entree:	1/2 lb crab meat	1/4 t salt
	1/2 head iceberg lettuce	1/2 cup mayonnaise
	1 cucumber	1 T sweet pickle relish
	2 hard-boiled eggs	1 t lemon juice
	2 tomatoes	
Bread:	French bread	
	Butter	
Dessert:	1 pkg instant lemon pudding	

1. Prepare crab meat.
2. Shred lettuce and place in large shallow salad bowls. Sprinkle lightly with salt. **HERS**
3. Arrange crab meat on lettuce.
4. Around edge of crab meat, place alternate slices of cucumber, tomato, and eggs.
5. Prepare dressing by combining 1/2 cup mayonnaise, 1 1/2 T ketchup, 1 T sweet pickle relish, 1 T lemon juice, and mixing thoroughly.
6. Spread dressing over salad just before serving.

ZESTY POTATO CHOWDER A LA CRAB
HOT BUTTERED FRENCH BREAD
HONEYDEW MELON WITH FRESH BLUEBERRIES

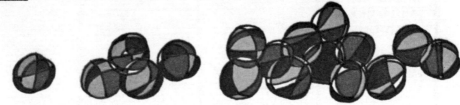

HIS

1. Set table.
2. Slice loaf of French bread in half — vertically; wrap half in foil and place in freezer. Slice other half vertically in diagonal cuts almost to bottom crust and place pats of butter between each cut. Wrap in foil, ready to place in oven.
3. Place bread in oven when partner adds last ingredient to chowder.
4. Remove the bread and serve with chowder.

Entree: 1 1/2 cups instant potatoes
         1 6-1/2 oz can crab meat
         1 T finely chopped parsley
         1 small can sliced mushrooms
         1 1/2 cups milk (or half-and-half)
         1 T instant minced onion
Bread: French bread
         Butter
Dessert: 1 honeydew melon   1/2 pint blueberries

1. Preheat oven to 300^0.
2. Prepare potatoes according to directions on package. Chop parsley while heating water or milk.
3. Gradually stir in milk until mixture is like cream soup.
4. Add crab meat, mushrooms, onion, and parsley. Season with salt to taste and freshly ground pepper.
5. Heat thoroughly and slowly. Do not boil.
6. Prepare melon wedges, gently rinse blueberries and refrigerate both until dessert time.

HERS

CRAB QUICHE
PAN-FRIED APPLE SLICES
LEMON SHERBET

HIS

1. Set table.
2. Preheat oven to 425°.
3. Wash apples and remove core. Slice, leaving peel on.
4. When partner reduces oven heat for quiche, melt butter in a medium skillet. Add apples and sprinkle with brown sugar, cinnamon, and nutmeg.
5. Cover pan; simmer over very low heat until apples are tender. Stir occasionally. If apples are ready before the quiche, don't panic. Just turn off the heat and leave the pan covered.
6. Serve sherbet.

Entree:	1 unbaked pie shell	3 eggs
	3/4 cup shredded Swiss cheese	Freshly ground pepper
	2 eggs & 3/4 cup milk	1/3 cup white wine
	3/4 t salt	1 6-1/2 oz can crab meat
Fruit:	2 apples	
	2 T butter or margarine	1/2 t cinnamon
	1 1/2 T brown sugar	1/4 t nutmeg
Dessert:	1 pint lemon sherbet	

HERS

1. Prepare pastry shell.
2. Drain crab meat and arrange pieces in pastry shell.
3. Sprinkle cheese over crab meat.
4. Beat eggs lightly, stir in milk, wine, salt and pepper.
5. Pour mixture over cheese and sprinkle with paprika.
6. Place below center of oven for 10 minutes; set timer.
7. Reduce heat to 350° when timer rings and bake for 25 minutes more or until center is "set".
8. Cool 10 minutes before cutting. Serve in wedges.

The ability to utilize menus from other # Foreign Night In
lands and cultures is often somewhat limited
by the availability of ingredients, depending
somewhat on where you live. If you reside in
a large metropolitan area, chances are you will
have no problem finding a specialty food store
which carries the more exotic and unusual imported foods. However, many Americans do
not have access to these shops; therefore I have

tried to provide menus which retain the authenticity of flavor but can be created
from readily available ingredients.

When preparing these menus, try to duplicate the atmosphere of the land
whose cuisine you are sampling. If you choose a Japanese menu, toss the pillows
on the floor and eat from a low table. Recordings of music native to a country
can contribute a great deal to atmosphere, as well as incense, flower arrange-
ments, even a small national flag in the center of the table.

Exploring the world through meal variation can be very exciting. Certainly
you will want to go beyond the menus offered here — they are intended only as
an introduction to world cuisine.

**PETE'S TOSTADAS
FRESH SLICED PEACHES
WITH CREAM**

Put some "south of the border" recordings on the stereo and settle down to this easy to prepare, yet authentic dinner from Mexico.

HIS

1. Prepare meat filling by browning ground beef in very small bits. Push meat to one side and saute onions lightly; mix with meat and add seasonings.
2. Heat refried beans.
3. Fry tortillas in cooking oil until crisp. Drain on paper towels.
4. Place 1 tortilla on each plate and each build your own tostada. First: Spread with refried beans, then meat filling, lettuce, tomatoes, onions and sauce.

Tostadas: 1 pkg tortillas
             1 lb ground beef
             1 onion
             Salt and pepper
             1 can refried beans
             1/4 t chili powder
             1/4 head iceberg lettuce, shredded
             1 tomato, cut in wedges
             Chili sauce
Dessert: 2 fresh peaches, sliced
             1/2 pint cream

1. Shred lettuce.
2. Chop onion and tomato.
3. Set table.
4. Slice peaches; refrigerate.

HERS

99

**CURRIED CHICKEN
RICE WITH ALMONDS
GARLIC SPINACH
ARAB RICE PUDDING**

The title "Arabian Night In" conjures up visions of softly lighted harem rooms, incense, silks, and beautiful veiled young ladies --- at least for the male contingent of American society. Set the scene as you wish, but the objective of meal preparation should be kept firmly in mind!

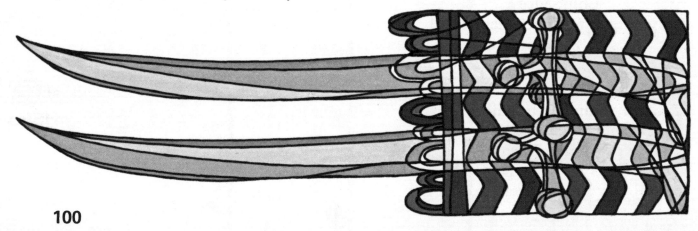

Entree:	1 T caraway seeds	1/4 t salt
	2 T Madras curry	1 t cayenne
	3/4 cup chopped onion	1 8-oz can stewed tomatoes
	2 garlic cloves	1 6-oz can tomato puree
	2 T butter	2 1/2 lb chicken, cut up

Rice: 1 pkg Green Giant rice with almonds

Spinach: 1 lb fresh spinach

1 onion

1/8 cup olive oil

1 lemon

1 garlic clove

Freshly ground pepper

Dessert: 2 cups milk

1/4 cup sugar

1/8 cup raw rice (plain short-grain)

HIS

1. Crush caraway seeds, add to curry and mix.
2. Finely chop 3/4 cup onion and 1 clove garlic.
3. Saute onion and garlic in 2 T butter, using a 3-quart saucepan.
4. Add curry-caraway mixture, salt, cayenne, tomatoes, and tomato puree. Simmer for 20 minutes over low heat, stirring occasionally.
5. Add pieces of chicken, cover and simmer until meat begins to loosen from bones - about 30 minutes. (If sauce becomes too thick, add a little hot water.) Set timer for 20 minutes and make progress check when it rings.
6. Wash spinach - - - - - THOROUGHLY!
7. Serve curry.
8. Serve dessert.

For a touch of authenticity, try serving with no silverware, just slices of soft fresh bread (with an assist from your fingers!) to scoop up the food. A couple of hot damp towels should be kept handy!

HERS

1. Put milk in a heavy saucepan and allow to come to a boil over low heat. Add rice and lower heat just as low as possible. Stir occasionally as mixture thickens.
2. When rice has dissolved into the milk, add sugar and continue to simmer and stir for about 8 minutes, then pour into dessert dishes. Chill.
3. When 15 minutes remain on the timer, begin preparation of rice with almonds according to package directions.
4. Set table.
5. Slice small onion and 1 garlic clove into skillet with olive oil. Saute until soft.
6. Add spinach and simmer until liquid cooks out and spinach is coated with oil. Season with salt, freshly ground pepper, and lemon juice. Serve.
7. Serve rice and almonds.

STEAKS POLYNESIAN
CHILLED GRAPES
RICE
PINEAPPLE SUNDAE

Entree: 4 frozen cube steaks
1 T butter
1 T minced onion
1/2 green pepper, seeded and cut in strips
Salt and pepper
1 small can sliced pineapple
1/4 cup soy sauce
2 T brown sugar
1 t finely sliced candied ginger
(or 1/2 t ground ginger)
1 1/2 T cornstarch
1/4 cup cold water

Rice: 2 servings minute rice

Fruit: 1 1/2 cups grapes, washed, removed from stems and chilled

Dessert: 1 pint vanilla ice cream
Pineapple sundae topping
Macadamia nuts

105

HIS

1. Remove grapes from stem, wash, refrigerate.
2. Crush a few Macadamia nuts for dessert topping.
3. Set table.
4. Prepare 2 servings of minute rice according to package directions.
5. Serve grapes.
6. Serve rice.
7. Serve dessert.
(Remember the atmosphere - - try a recording of Hawaiian music on the stereo!)

HERS

1. Prepare minced onion and green pepper strips.
2. Melt 1 T butter in skillet and brown steaks quickly.
3. Add onion, green pepper, salt and freshly ground pepper to skillet, and saute lightly.
4. Add pineapple slices and juice, soy sauce, brown sugar, and ginger. Heat thoroughly over low heat.
5. While the above mixture is heating, blend cornstarch to a smooth paste with the water.
6. Arrange the meat, pineapple slices, and pepper strips on a hot platter. Stir cornstarch mixture into the hot liquid in skillet, stirring constantly, until sauce thickens and clears. Pour sauce over steaks.

HUNGARIAN GOULASH
BUTTERED NOODLES
BRUSSELS SPROUTS
APPLE STRUDEL

Goulash is probably the best known dish from Hungary which has been adapted to American menus. However, there are many other delicious concoctions imported from that country which you may wish to learn about after preparing this flavorful meal.

Entree:	1/2 lb round steak
	1/2 lb veal steak
	1/2 lb pork shoulder
	Salt and pepper
	1/2 cup chopped onion
	1 garlic clove
	1/4 cup shortening
	1/2 t caraway seeds
	1 1/2 T paprika
	2 fresh tomatoes
	1 small green pepper
Noodles:	1 box egg noodles
	1 T butter
Vegetable:	1 pkg frozen brussels sprouts
	1 T butter
	2 green onions
	2 T sour cream
	Dash paprika
Dessert:	2 servings apple strudel from your local bakery.

 **HIS**

1. Chop onion and garlic; crush caraway seeds.
2. Seed green pepper and slice into thin strips.
3. Chop tomatoes into eighths - or chunks.
4. Set table.
5. When timer is set for second time, cook sprouts according to directions.
6. Start noodles according to preparation time on package so they will be ready when goulash is done. When cooked, drain and add butter and seasoning.
7. Chop green onions.
8. Serve noodles.
9. Serve dessert.

HERS

1. Cut meat into 1-inch cubes and salt them. Using a heavy saucepan, melt shortening and saute onion and garlic.
2. Add caraway seeds and paprika. Stir; add cubes and cover pan. Reduce heat to low. Set timer for 45 minutes.
3. When timer rings, add tomatoes and green pepper and set timer for another 45 minutes.
4. When brussel sprouts are cooked and drained, melt 1 T butter in skillet. Saute green onions and add them to the sprouts.
5. Fold in the sour cream just before the goulash will be done; place over low heat - **DO NOT BOIL!** Place in serving dish and sprinkle with paprika.
6. Serve goulash.

This meal requires about 2 hours preparation time from start to finish. You will probably prefer to have this foreign meal on a weekend - - unless you like to occasionally dine fashionably late!

CHICKEN CACCIATORE
ANTIPASTO TRAY
ROMAINE SALAD
HOT BUTTERED FRENCH BREAD
RED WINE AND DESSERT CHEESES

Antipasto: From your delicatessen, select the items for your antipasto tray: delicate slices of salami, marinated garbanzo beans, thin slices of cheeses of your choice; fresh vegetables - if you please. It's up to you!

Entree:
1 1/2 lbs chicken, cut up
(or 4 chicken breasts)
1/3 cup olive oil
1/4 cup dry red wine
1/2 green pepper, in strips or chopped
1 small can sliced mushrooms, drained

1/4 cup minced onion
1 clove garlic, minced
1 can tomato soup or
1 1/2 cups stewed tomatoes
1/4 cup water

Salad:
1/2 t oregano
1 head Romaine lettuce

Italian dressing

Bread:
1 T Parmesan cheese

French bread

Dessert:
1/4 cup butter

Red dinner wine and dessert cheese

113

 HIS

1. Wash the romaine lettuce, pat dry with paper towels, and place in the crisper drawer of refrigerator.
2. Set table.
3. When chicken has been covered and left to simmer, split and butter the French bread (sprinkle with Parmesan cheese if you like), wrap in foil and set aside for placing in the oven when about 8 minutes are left on the timer.
4. Prepare antipasto tray.
5. Wash dessert grapes (do not remove from stems) and place on dessert plates along with wedges of the dessert cheese. Refrigerate until dessert time.
6. Remember to put French bread in oven.
7. Serve antipasto tray.
8. When timer rings for chicken, add dressing to lettuce (put it in a salad bowl first!) and toss. Sprinkle with Parmesan cheese and serve.
9. Serve French bread.

HERS

1. Marinate chicken for 30 minutes in equal parts wine and water to cover - if time allows.
2. Drain, place in skillet in which olive oil has been heated and brown chicken on all sides.
3. Add onion, green pepper, mushrooms, garlic, tomatoes (or soup), wine, and water. Add seasonings, stir, and reduce heat to low.
4. Cover and simmer, stirring occasionally for about 30 minutes or until meat begins to loosen from bones.
5. Remove chicken to serving dish and spoon sauce over chicken. If desired, rice can be prepared and the sauce spooned over the rice as a side dish.
6. Serve dessert.

SIMPLE TERIYAKI
FRIED NOODLES
CORN ON THE COB
FRESH APPLE SLICES

This menu is adapted from the Japanese Country Cookbook by Russ Rudzinski.

The usual comment about the Japanese Country Cookbook is "by Rudzinski?". Actually, Russ lived for many years in Japan and is married to a very lovely Japanese lady named Miyo. Together they own and operate an excellent San Francisco restaurant, the Mingei-ya.

Entree:	Fish for two, fillets or whole
	Soy sauce
	Vegetable oil
Noodles:	2 servings cooked noodles (soba, a Japanese noodle or Tagliatelle noodles)
	1 T vegetable oil
	2 t soy sauce
	1 T chopped green onions
	Freshly ground pepper
Vegetable:	4 ears corn
	Soy sauce
Dessert:	2 apples

1. Prepare enough noodles for 2 servings. Add 1 T cooking oil to prevent sticking.
2. Set table.
3. Put on large pan half full of hot water over medium heat for corn. Add 1 T salt.
4. When noodles are done, drain. Place 1 T oil in skillet over medium heat, add noodles, and mix gently until heated through. Add onions, mix, sprinkle with freshly ground pepper and serve.
5. As soon as water is boiling, drop in corn (husked, please!), bring to a boil again, cover, and boil for 5 minutes. Remove and brush with soy sauce. Serve.

HERS

1. Preheat broiler.
2. Combine about 2 T soy sauce and 2 T cooking oil in small bowl. Brush mixture on fish.
3. Place fish under broiler. Turn every 4 minutes using a broad spatula to prevent breaking the fish - and brush with soy sauce mixture each time until edges are getting crispy and center flakes when pierced with a fork.
4. While fish is broiling, slice and core apples (do not peel) and place in a bowl of slightly salted cold water to keep them fresh-looking. Place on table for dessert.
5. Serve teriyaki.

**CALVES LIVER WITH
SAUCE BERCY
BUTTERED ASPARAGUS
RICE
LETTUCE SALAD WITH BLEU CHEESE DRESSING
BRANDIED PEARS WITH ICE CREAM**

Liver can be elegant, particularly if it is not overcooked. Here is an inexpensive gourmet meal that can transport you - in imagination - to the heart of Paris. If you both "parler Francais", do so!

Entree:	1 lb calves liver
	2 T butter
	Salt and freshly ground pepper
Sauce Bercy:	1 green onion, chopped
	1/3 cup dry white wine
	1 1/2 T butter
	1 T lemon juice
	1 t parsley, chopped
	Salt and freshly ground pepper
Rice:	2 servings prepared according to package directions
Salad:	1/2 head iceberg lettuce
	Bleu cheese dressing
Dessert:	1 pint vanilla ice cream
	1 jar (small) brandied pears

 **HIS**

1. Cook asparagus according to package directions.
2. Mince onion and combine with 1/3 cup wine in saucepan; simmer until wine is reduced by about half.
3. Chop parsley.
4. Add 2 T butter to onions, stir until melted, then add 1 T lemon juice and parsley. Season with salt and pepper. Heat but do not boil.
5. Add dressing to salad and serve.
6. Serve asparagus.
7. Put ice cream in dessert dishes, place a brandied pear on each side of ice cream and serve.

HERS

1. Set table.
2. Prepare 2 servings of minute rice.
3. Wash and chop lettuce; refrigerate. Add dressing just before serving.
4. Melt 1 1/2 T butter in heavy skillet. Season the liver with salt and pepper; place in skillet. Saute quickly - about 3 minutes to a side. **DO NOT OVERCOOK!**
5. Serve liver topped with sauce.
6. Add butter and fluff rice with a fork just before serving.

CHINESE SUPPER WITH RICE
FRESH FRUIT AND
FORTUNE COOKIES
TEA

Entree: 1/3 lb raw shrimp, shelled and de-veined
1/3 lb ground lean pork
1 T peanut oil (or cooking oil)
1/4 cup finely chopped scallions
3/4 cup chicken bouillon
1 1/2 t soy sauce
1 pkg frozen snow peas
Rice: 2 servings minute rice
Dessert: Melon, oranges, or apples
Fortune cookies

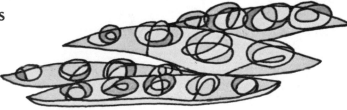

HIS

1. Rinse shrimp, cut in halves lengthwise.
2. Chop scallions and slice mushrooms.
3. Combine bouillon and soy sauce in measuring cup.
4. Prepare rice according to directions.
5. Prepare fruit.
6. Heat water for tea and make tea.
7. Serve tea.
8. Serve fruit for dessert with fortune cookies.

HERS

1. Set <u>low</u> table.
2. In 1 T peanut oil, fry pork, stirring to break into small bits.
3. Add shrimp and scallions; Chinese-fry (stir-fry) for 2 minutes.
4. Add snow peas and mix gently. Turn up heat.
5. Cook 3 minutes or until snow peas are thawed but still crisp.
6. Serve over rice.

STUFFED PEPPERS WITH
YOGURT DRESSING
VEGETABLE SALAD
APPLE COMPOTE

TURKISH NIGHT IN

Dim the lights, put on your long flowing robes, take the cushions off the couch, place them on the floor around the coffee table and enjoy your Turkish Night In. To be authentic, eat this entire meal with your hands, as the Turkish people do not use any utensils.

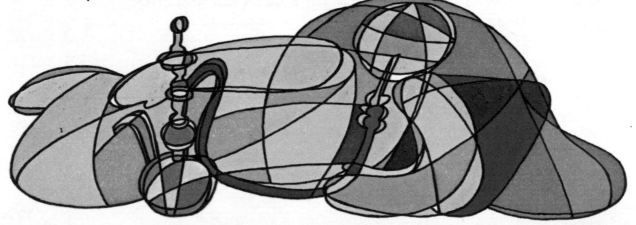

Entree:	4 medium bell peppers	
	1/2 cup water	
	1/4 cup tomato puree	
Meat Filling:	1 lb ground sirloin	1/8 t dill weed
	2 T butter	3/4 cup water
	1 medium onion	Salt and pepper
	1/4 cup converted rice	
Salad:	1 onion	1 T chopped parsley
	1/2 green pepper	1 T olive oil
	2 tomatoes	1 T lemon juice
	1/2 cucumber	
Yogurt Dressing:	1/4 lb yogurt	
	1/8 cup water	
	Dash garlic salt	
Dessert:	2 apples	
	1/2 cup water	
	1/2 cup sugar	

HIS

1. Prepare meat filling by sauteing onion in 2 T butter until transparent; add rice and stir to coat with butter. Add 3/4 cup water, bring to a boil; reduce heat to low, cover, and simmer until rice is tender and fluffy. All water should be absorbed.
2. Remove from heat, uncover to cool.
3. Add ground meat, dill weed, salt, pepper and mix well.
4. Spoon filling into peppers loosely, place open end up in deep pan (preferably a Dutch oven), and pour tomato puree mixture over top of peppers.
5. Place over low heat to simmer for 30 minutes. Add water occasionally if bottom of pan becomes dry. Set timer.
6. Combine 1/4 lb yogurt, 1/8 cup water, and dash of garlic salt. Spoon over stuffed peppers just before serving.

1. Cut off top of peppers and scoop out seeds and fibers. Rinse peppers inside to remove all seeds.
2. Place in pan of boiling salted water for 5 minutes; drain and put on paper towels to cool. Use tongs - gently - to remove from pan.
3. Combine 1/2 cup water and 1/4 cup tomato puree for partner.
4. Set table.
5. Cut onion sideways to form crescents, peel and chop tomatoes, chop green pepper and cucumber. Combine all and toss gently to mix.
6. Combine olive oil and lemon juice. Pour over salad just before serving. Garnish salad with chopped parsley.
7. Combine 1/2 cup sugar and 1/2 cup water in small saucepan. Boil for 5 minutes.
8. Peel, core and slice apples and poach in the syrup, a few slices at a time, until slices are transparent. Place in dessert dishes as they are done. When all slices are cooked, pour a little of the remaining syrup over each serving.
9. Serve salad.
10. Serve dessert.

HERS

When "gourmet" cooking is mentioned, often the mental image of an excellent, flavorful meal is clouded a bit by the recollection of stacks of dirty pots and pans, expensive hard - to - find ingredients, and possibly a touch of indigestion from too-rich sauces and seasonings.

Not necessarily so. Today's convenience foods can provide shortcuts (and fewer pots and pans!) without losing the authenticity of the original recipe.

The Weekend

Gourmet

Gourmet meals are prepared by using creative flair and imagination in preparing foods which are already familiar to you. Many creative cooks have contributed their unique touches to lift everyday fare to the level of haute cuisine. Feel free to add individual touches, governed by your own likes and dislikes. If "HE" wants to add some oregano and "SHE" thinks good old chopped parsley will do the trick, try both — or prepare it on two different occasions, once a la oregano and once a la parsley.

**VEAL CURRY
RICE
CONDIMENTS**

The special, unique flavor of curry, combined with the extra fun of choosing your own selection of condiments makes your Veal Curry dinner a different and special occasion.

HIS

1. Cube veal; melt butter in medium-size skillet and brown veal. Turn off heat. Partner will add veal to sauce.
2. When about 10 minutes remain on timer, prepare rice.
3. Set table.
4. Serve rice.

134

Entree:	1 lb breast of veal, cubed	3/4 cup canned tomatoes
	2 T butter	3/4 cup bouillon
Sauce:	1/2 medium onion	1/2 apple
	1/2 medium carrot	1/2 T sweet pickle relish
	1/2 T curry powder	
	1 T butter	
	1 T flour	
Rice:	2 servings minute rice	
Condiments:	Minced olives, chopped cashews, chutney, grated coconut	

1. Slice onion and carrot; chop apple.
2. Make sauce by melting 1 T butter in skillet, saute sliced onion and carrot.
3. Add curry, mix, and stir in flour; add tomatoes, bouillon, apple, and pickle relish.
4. Simmer for five minutes.
5. Add browned veal and simmer, covered, for 45 minutes. Set timer.
6. Prepare condiments when about 10 minutes remain on timer.

HERS

VEAL PROVENCALE
WATERCRESS SALAD
SWEET-SOUR POTATOES
FIGS WITH WHIPPED CREAM

The French love veal, and you will too - when you've prepared this tender, tasty repast from France.

Entree:	1 fresh tomato	2 T butter
	1 lb veal cutlets (about 1/8-inch thick)	1/4 lb mushrooms
	1/4 t salt	1/3 cup white wine
	1/4 t freshly ground pepper	1 garlic clove
	1 T flour	
Salad:	1 bunch watercress	
	Vinegar and oil dressing	
Potatoes:	2 slices bacon	
	1 1/2 cups diced boiled potatoes (frozen may be used)	
	1/4 onion	
	1 t sugar	
	1/4 t salt	
	1/4 cup water	
	1/8 cup vinegar	
Dessert:	6 fresh figs	
	1/2 pint whipping cream	

 HIS

1. Set table.
2. Finely chop onion.
3. Wash watercress, remove stems, and refrigerate.
4. Peel tomato. If you have a gas stove, impale the tomato on a fork and hold it over the flame, rotating it slowly until the skin blisters. It's now easier to peel.
5. Chop tomato.
6. Dredge the veal in mixture of flour, salt and pepper.
7. Melt 2 T butter in skillet, add veal, and brown on both sides.
8. Wash and stem mushrooms while veal is browning. When browned, add mushrooms to skillet and saute for 5 minutes.
9. Add tomatoes and garlic clove to skillet, cover and simmer about 10 minutes.
10. When veal and potatoes are ready, place veal on serving plate, add dressing to salad, toss, and serve veal and salad.

HERS

1. Fry 2 slices bacon in skillet until crisp; remove from pan, drain on paper towel, and crumble.
2. Using 1 T of bacon drippings, fry potatoes over medium heat, without turning, until brown on the bottom (about 10 - 15 minutes). Turn, add onion and cook 5 minutes more.
3. Sprinkle sugar and salt over potatoes, add water, cover and simmer for about 15 minutes. Set timer.
4. Wash figs and remove stems.
5. Whip cream, adding 1 t sugar when cream first begins to thicken. Refrigerate.
6. Make dressing of 1 T vinegar, 2 T olive oil, 1/2 t salt and 1/2 t freshly ground pepper. Refrigerate.
7. Serve potatoes when partner says veal is ready. If both veal and potatoes are not ready at the same time - either can simmer a bit longer without suffering loss of edibility or flavor.
8. Serve figs topped with whipped cream and a dash of nutmeg.

139

SHRIMP SCAMPI
GREEN SALAD WITH FRENCH DRESSING
CHEDDAR POTATOES
LEMONY NECTARINES

Entree:
16 fresh shrimp
4 cloves garlic
1/4 cup olive oil
3 T butter

1 T chopped parsley
1/2 t salt
Freshly ground pepper
Parsley for garnish

Potatoes:
2 large potatoes
1 egg yolk
1/2 cup milk
1/2 cup grated Cheddar cheese

Salad:
Salad greens
French dressing

Schilling's Salad Supreme seasoning
Butter

Dessert:
3 nectarines
4 T lemonade
2 T slivered almonds

HIS

1. Preheat oven to 325º.
2. Scrub potatoes, remove "eyes", rub with shortening, puncture skins with fork in 4 or 5 places, wrap in foil, and place in oven. Set timer for 1 hour.
3. Prepare salad greens and refrigerate.
4. When timer rings, adjust oven temperature to 350º, remove potatoes from oven, open foil and fold back. Slit skins and scoop out centers.
5. Sieve or mash scooped out portions to a coarse consistency.
6. Beat egg yolk, salt, and pepper together; combine with potato and mix well.
7. Return potato mixture to shell and spread cheese over top. Sprinkle with Salad Supreme Seasoning, dot with butter and return to oven until lightly browned (about 10 - 15 minutes).
8. Add dressing to greens and toss lightly when shrimp and potatoes are almost ready.

HERS

1. Set table.
2. Peel and slice nectarines and arrange in dessert dishes. Spoon 2 T lemonade over each; refrigerate.
3. Remove shells from shrimp and de-vein, rinsing under cold tap water. Drain on paper towels.
4. Mince 4 cloves of garlic.
5. When 10 minutes remain on 2nd setting of timer for potatoes, place heavy skillet over medium-high heat. Add 1/4 cup olive oil and 3 T butter; when hot, add shrimp.
6. Cook about 3 minutes, stirring often.
7. Add garlic, parsley, and salt. Cook for 2 minutes, stirring often. Place on serving plate, spoon sauce over all and serve. Garnish with parsley.
8. Serve nectarines for dessert.

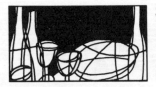

SHORT RIBS IN BURGUNDY
FLORENTINE SALAD
FRENCH ROLLS PARMESAN
MINTED PEACHES

Short ribs are a tasty and economical cut of beef and you will find this a most delicious method of preparation. The Florentine Salad is quite unique and loaded with vitamins. You may wish to substitute this salad in other menus.

Entree:	1 1/2 lb short ribs	2 T instant minced onion
	1/2 cup burgundy wine	1 1/4 t salt
	1 small can tomato sauce	2 T red wine vinegar
	1 t brown sugar	1/4 t paprika
Salad:	2 cloves garlic	
	3/4 lb fresh spinach	
	2 hard-boiled eggs	
	3 slices bacon	
	1/3 cup salad oil	
	2 1/2 T vinegar	
Bread:	2 French rolls	
	Butter	
	Parmesan cheese	
Dessert:	1 small can sliced peaches	
	1/4 cup crushed peppermint candy	
	2 (drops red food coloring)	

 HIS

1. Rub skillet or Dutch oven with oil and heat. Brown short ribs on all sides; drain off excess grease.
2. Combine wine, tomato sauce, onion, salt, paprika and vinegar; pour over browned ribs.
3. Cover tightly, place in oven and bake for 1 hour and 45 minutes. Use timer.
4. Using a small saucepan, immerse 2 eggs in water and place over medium heat. When water begins to bubble, reduce heat to low and simmer for 10 minutes. Remove from heat, drain, and place under cold running water for 3 minutes.
5. When 5 minutes remain on timer for ribs, split French rolls, butter, and sprinkle liberally with Parmesan cheese.
6. When ribs are removed from oven, adjust temperature to 375° and place rolls in oven to heat.
7. Place ribs in deep serving dish and spoon juices over them.   Serve.
8. Remove rolls from oven and serve.

HERS

1. Preheat oven to 300°.
2. Open peaches and drain syrup into small saucepan. Place peach slices in dessert dishes.
3. Add crushed candy to syrup plus 2 drops red food coloring.
4. Simmer and stir until candy dissolves. Pour over peach slices and refrigerate.
5. Wash spinach, remove stems, tear leaves into bite-size pieces. Pat dry with paper towels and refrigerate.
6. Place 1 clove of garlic in 1/3 cup oil and refrigerate.
7. Fry bacon until crisp. Drain on paper towel.
8. When a few minutes remain on timer for ribs, remove garlic clove from oil and combine oil with 2 1/2 T vinegar, 1/4 t salt, 1/2 t freshly ground pepper and place in large salad bowl. Add spinach and toss.
9. Chop eggs, crumble bacon and sprinkle both over spinach. Toss again and serve.
10. Serve dessert.

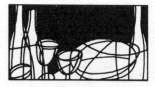

CHICKEN MAXIMILLIAN
PARSLIED CARROTS
POPOVERS
CAKE AND ICE CREAM ROLL

This elegant chicken entree is greatly enhanced by its original cooking sauce. In this menu, the inexpensive becomes a gourmet treat.

Entree:	2 chicken breasts
	1/2 t salt
	1/4 t paprika
	3 T butter
	1 T slivered orange rind
	1/3 cup orange juice
	1 t instant minced onion
	1/4 t ginger
	1 t cornstarch
	1 avocado
Vegetable:	2 medium carrots
	2 T butter
	1 t chopped parsley
	Salt and pepper
Bread:	1 egg
	1/2 cup milk
	1/2 cup flour
	1/8 t salt
Dessert:	Frozen cake and ice cream roll

 **HIS**

1. Preheat oven to 400°.
2. Prepare popovers by placing all ingredients in a bowl and beating until smooth. If you have a blender, place all ingredients in the blender and mix.
3. Generously grease 6 muffin cups in a muffin tin and fill each cup half full with the popover batter.
4. When oven is preheated, place pan in oven and set timer for 40 minutes.
5. Scrape, wash and cut carrots into thin slices.
6. Melt butter in skillet using medium heat. Add carrots and cook until soft, about 15 minutes. Add parsley, salt and pepper. Serve.
7. Set table.
8. Peel avocado and cut into wedges.
9. Serve popovers.

150

HERS

1. Sprinkle chicken breasts on each side with salt and paprika.
2. Melt butter in skillet and brown the chicken on both sides.
3. Add orange rind, juice, onion, and ginger.
4. Cover, reduce heat to low, and cook for 30 minutes or until chicken is tender.
5. Remove chicken and place on heated platter.
6. Blend cornstarch with a little cold water to make a smooth paste. Stir into the sauce in the skillet. Cook until mixture thickens and comes to a boil.
7. Arrange avocado wedges around chicken on the platter and pour a small amount of sauce over the chicken. Put remaining sauce into a small bowl.
8. Serve chicken and sauce.
9. Serve dessert.

151

FISH ROLLADES WITH SHRIMP NEWBURG SAUCE
WILD RICE
FRENCH BEANS AMANDINE
VANILLA ICE CREAM WITH BRANDIED CHERRIES

Entree:
4 fish fillets (about 1 lb)
5 T butter
1/8 t nutmeg
2 T paprika
2 T flour
1/4 t salt

1/8 t Tabasco sauce
1/2 cup milk
1 egg yolk
1/4 cup half-and-half
1/3 lb cooked, cleaned shrimp
2 T sherry

Rice:
1 pkg Rice-a-roni wild rice

Vegetable:
1 pkg frozen french beans
1/2 cup slivered blanched almonds

Dessert:
1 pint vanilla ice cream
1 can pitted black cherries
2 T brandy

HIS

1. Preheat oven to 400°.
2. Cook french beans according to package directions.
3. Melt 2 T butter (use same saucepan partner used!) and add almonds. Saute over low heat until brown, stirring frequently. When brown, turn off heat and add them to the beans just before serving.
4. Separate one egg yolk from the white and beat yolk together with half-in-half.
5. Put cherries in small saucepan, add brandy. Heat just before serving dessert.
6. Set table.
7. Combine almonds and beans, add salt and freshly ground pepper, and serve.
8. Serve Rice-a-roni while partner serves fillets and sauce.
9. Serve dessert.

NOTE: For a quick Shrimp sauce, combine 1 10-oz can frozen cream of shrimp soup (condensed), 1/3 cup half-and-half and 1/4 t Tabasco sauce, and heat.

154

HERS

1. Sprinkle fillets on both sides with salt, roll up from narrow end and place - "seam" side down - in shallow baking pan.
2. Melt 2 T butter in small saucepan and drizzle or brush over fillets, sprinkle with paprika, and place in oven. Set timer for 20 minutes.
3. Cook Rice-a-roni wild rice according to package directions.
4. Melt 1 T butter in saucepan, add 2 T flour, 1/4 t salt, 1/8 t nutmeg and 1/8 t Tabasco sauce.
5. Stir in 1/2 cup milk, and place over medium heat, stirring constantly until mixture thickens and comes to a boil.
6. Reduce heat to low and stir in egg yolk mixture partner has prepared.
7. Add shrimp and keep over low heat until shrimp is heated through - DO NOT BOIL! Stir in sherry.
8. Serve shrimp sauce over fish fillets.

BEEF BURGUNDY WITH NOODLES
TOSSED GREEN SALAD
SPICED PEACHES
STRAWBERRY SHERBET

You will find a number of menus included in "Working Couples" which require wine in the preparation of the entree. Cooking with wine adds a whole new dimension and flavor to your cuisine. The American wines are comparable in flavor, bouquet and texture to the most famous wines of France - so cooking with wine need not be exclusive to the table of the wealthy gourmet.

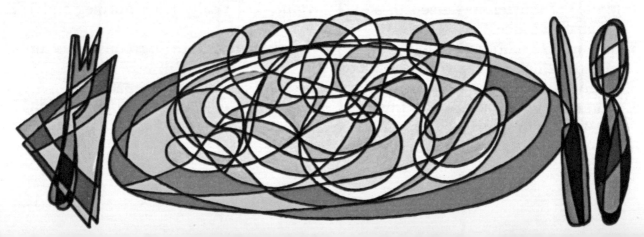

Entree:	3/4 lb round steak
	1 T flour
	1 T butter
	2 T chopped onion
	1 t chopped parsley
	1/2 clove garlic, chopped
	1/2 bay leaf
	1/4 t salt
	1/4 t freshly ground pepper
	1 3-oz can sliced mushrooms, drained
	1/3 cup burgundy wine
	1/3 cup water
	2 servings egg noodles
Salad:	Greens of your choice
	French dressing
Condiment:	1 small jar spiced peaches
Dessert:	1 pint strawberry sherbet

HIS

1. Chop onion, parsley and garlic.
2. Set table.
3. When about 30 minutes remain on timer, put pan of hot salted water — adding 1 t cooking oil — over medium heat for cooking noodles.
4. Cook noodles according to package directions, enough for 2 servings.
5. Open spiced peaches and place 4 or 5 in small serving dish.
6. Prepare greens for salad.
7. When noodles are done, drain and place one serving on each plate when entree is ready to serve.
8. Put dressing on salad and toss.

HERS

1. Cut steak into 1-inch cubes, dredge in flour — using the entire T of flour.
2. Melt 1 T butter in skillet, add steak cubes, and brown on all sides.
3. Turn off heat, add onion, parsley, garlic, 1/2 bay leaf, 1/4 t salt and 1/4 t freshly ground pepper.
4. Stir in mushrooms (drained), 1/3 cup burgundy and 1/3 cup water. Mix well and turn on heat to bring to a boil.
5. Reduce heat to low and simmer, covered, about 50-60 minutes. Set timer for 50 minutes and check.
6. When done, retrieve bay leaf — if you can find it! If you can't — c'est la vie.
7. Serve steak over noodles.
8. Serve dessert.

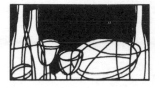

ASPARAGUS WITH LOBSTER SAUCE
APRICOT NECTAR
SLICED TOMATOES
PARKER HOUSE ROLLS
GRAPES DANTAS

Appetizer:	2 small cans apricot nectar
Entree:	1 frozen lobster tail (about 8 oz)
	10 medium asparagus spears
	3 T butter
	1 1/2 T brandy
	1/3 cup heavy cream
Vegetable:	2 medium tomatoes
Bread:	6 small Parker House rolls
	Butter
Dessert:	1 1/2 cup seedless grapes
	2/3 cup sour cream
	1/4 cup brown sugar
	Dash nutmeg

 HIS

1. Boil lobster tail in salted water according to package directions.
2. Remove meat from shell, slice into 6 pieces, and place in covered dish to keep warm.
3. Wash and trim asparagus spears; lay them flat and parallel in a wide shallow pan with just enough boiling salted water to cover. (Try a pair of tongs for arranging spears in the hot water.)
4. Cook until tender when pierced with a fork. Remove from heat and drain.
5. Melt 4 T butter in large skillet, add asparagus, and shake pan gently to rotate spears. Do not saute. Gently lift spears using a spatula and arrange 5 spears on each serving plate.
6. Heat the lobster slices in same pan, turning them once. Pour the brandy over lobster, flaming it as you finish. Arrange lobster slices on the asparagus.
7. Add 1/3 cup heavy cream to same pan and boil — it will thicken rapidly. Pour this sauce over the lobster and asparagus and serve.

HERS

1. Remove grapes from stem, rinse, and drain on paper towels.
2. Combine sour cream and brown sugar and mix well. Add grapes, fold into sour cream mixture, and chill.
3. Preheat oven to 250°.
4. Set table. Keep serving plates in kitchen, in a warm place if possible.
5. Arrange Parker House rolls on a baking sheet.
6. Slice tomatoes (or quarter them, if you prefer) and place in serving dish.
7. When partner removes asparagus from skillet, put rolls in oven to heat.
8. Serve apricot nectar.
9. Serve rolls and tomato slices.
10. Serve dessert.

PORK AND VEAL EN BROCHETTE
FRENCH ONION SOUP
TOMATO WEDGES
MASHED POTATOES
PEAS WITH SCALLIONS
LEMON SHERBET

This entree is a variation of the usual skewered barbecued cubes of meat. The pork and veal will cook thoroughly at about the same rate and they make a delicious combination.

Soup:	1 pkg Lipton's French onion soup	Cooking oil
	Parmesan cheese	1 t salt
Entree:	1/2 lb veal steak	1/4 cup water
	1/8 lb fresh pork steak	1/4 cup sour cream
	1 egg	
	1/2 cup corn flake crumbs	
Potatoes:	2 servings instant mashed potatoes	
	Salt, pepper, and butter	
Vegetable:	1 tomato, cut in wedges	
Vegetable:	1 pkg frozen peas	
	3 scallions, finely chopped	
	1 T butter	
	3 small lettuce leaves, shredded	
	1/2 t sugar	
	1/4 t salt	
Dessert:	1 pint lemon sherbet	

# HIS

1. Cut veal and pork into 1 1/2-inch cubes. Place 2 cubes of pork and 2 cubes of veal alternately on 4 skewers.
2. Dip each into beaten egg, then crumbs, and brown in skillet with heated cooking oil (about 1/4 cup).
3. Season with salt and pepper, add water, cover, and simmer about 1 hour. Set timer.
4. Prepare 2 servings mashed potatoes when about 8 minutes remain on timer.
5. Remove skewers to platter, pour off excess fat from skillet, add cream. Heat through and serve with meat.
6. Serve dessert.

HERS

1. Set table.
2. Prepare French onion soup. Sprinkle with Parmesan cheese after pouring into soup cups.
3. Wash tomatoes and cut into wedges.
4. Cook peas according to directions and drain.
5. Saute scallions in butter until soft; add lettuce leaves, sugar, and salt. Simmer for 5 minutes.
6. Add peas and simmer gently for 5 minutes more.
7. Serve soup sprinkled with Parmesan cheese.
8. Serve peas, tomato wedges, and potatoes.

BAHA CHICKEN ON RICE
FRENCH PEAS
STRAWBERRY MOUSSE

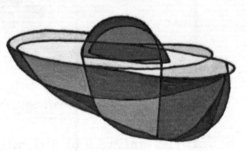

HIS

1 HOUR BEFORE PREPARATION TIME: Put chicken in large pan, cover with water, add 1 1/2 t salt, 1/2 t pepper, 1 stalk of celery, and 1 t minced onion. Cover and boil gently for 45 minutes. Drain, reserving 1 cup broth.

1. Remove skin and bones from chicken and cut into bite-size chunks.
2. Place peas, lettuce leaves, and 2 T sugar in small saucepan. Cover and simmer over low heat until ready to serve chicken.
3. Peel and dice avocado.
4. Set table.
5. Prepare 2 servings minute rice.
6. Serve peas.

Entree:	1 2-lb fryer, sectioned	1/4 cup flour
	Salt and pepper to taste	1/2 cup half-and-half
	2 diced pimientos	1/2 cup white wine
	1 stalk celery	1 small avocado
	1 t instant minced onion	1/4 cup toasted almonds
	1/3 cup butter	2 servings minute rice
	1 small can sliced mushrooms	
Vegetable:	1 pkg frozen peas	
	2 lettuce leaves	2 T sugar
Dessert:	See following pages for ingredients and preparation instructions for Strawberry Mousse.	

1. Open mushrooms, drain. Dice pimiento.
2. Melt butter in large skillet. Saute mushrooms lightly; blend in 1/4 cup flour, 3/4 t salt, and 1/4 t pepper, stirring constantly.
3. Slowly add 1 cup chicken broth. Simmer until sauce thickens.
4. Add chicken, half-and-half, and wine. Keep heat low.
5. When mixture is very hot, gently stir in diced avocado and almonds.
6. Serve over rice. If you prefer, may be served in patty shells, over noodles, or over half an avocado.

HERS

169

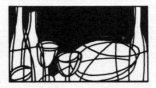

STRAWBERRY MOUSSE

1. Cut ice cream into chunks in medium size bowl.
2. Grate 3/4 T orange rind.
3. Have ring mold ready for partner to pour gelatin mixture into.
4. Thaw strawberries and drain off juice into small saucepan.
5. Blend in cornstarch and cook until sauce thickens, stirring constantly.
6. Cool. Add berries, stir, and chill.

170

1 pint strawberry ice cream
1 envelope unflavored gelatin
3/4 cup fresh orange juice
3/4 T grated orange rind
1 small pkg frozen strawberries
3/4 t cornstarch

1. Squeeze orange juice.
2. Put orange juice into small pan and sprinkle gelatin over it. Place over medium heat, stirring constantly until gelatin is dissolved.
3. Add orange rind and stir.
4. Pour hot mixture over softened ice cream and beat until blended. Pour quickly into 3-cup mold. Chill until set (about 1 hour).
5. When ready to serve dessert, unmold mousse and spoon sauce over it.

LAMB CHOPS EN CASSEROLE
BOILED NEW POTATOES
PARMESAN TOMATOES
PEACH MELBA

Entree:	4 lamb chops (1/2-inch thick)	1/2 t freshly ground pepper
	7 small pearl onions	1 clove garlic
	6 mushrooms, sliced	1 T fresh parsley, finely chopped
	1 1/4 T butter	1 cup frozen peas
	1/3 cup flour	1/2 cup bouillon
	1/2 t salt	
Potatoes:	6 new potatoes	1/2 t fresh parsley, chopped
	1 T butter	
Vegetable:	2 fresh tomatoes	
	Parmesan cheese	
Dessert:	1 pint vanilla ice cream	
	1 pkg red raspberries, thawed	
	1 small can peach halves	
	1/4 cup sugar	
	Dash cream of tartar	

HIS

1. Preheat oven to 300°.
2. Dissolve 1/2 bouillon cube in 1/3 cup of hot water.
3. Chop 1 1/2 T fresh parsley.
4. Half fill a 2-quart saucepan with hot water, adding 1 T salt, and place over high heat. When water is boiling - and chops have been placed in oven - add washed potatoes and cook uncovered for about 30 minutes or until done.
5. Slice tomatoes in half crosswise, sprinkle with Parmesan cheese and set in shallow baking dish. Place under broiler immediately upon removal of chops.
6. Set table.
7. Cook 1 cup peas in salted water.
8. Drain potatoes, dot with butter, stir to coat with butter, and sprinkle with remaining chopped parsley. Serve.
9. As soon as chops are removed from oven, turn on broiler and pop the tomatoes under the broiler. This takes about 4 minutes - - DON'T FORGET THEM!
10. Add peas to the casserole.
11. Serve broiled tomatoes.
12. Prepare dessert by placing a scoop of ice cream in each dessert dish, arrange a peach half on either side of ice cream and spoon the Melba sauce over all.

1. Peel onions and slice mushrooms.
2. Melt 1 1/4 T butter in large skillet. Add onions and mushrooms and saute for 6 minutes.
3. While the above are sauteing, combine 1/3 cup flour, 1/2 t salt and 1/2 t freshly ground pepper; mix and dredge lamb chops with the mixture.
4. Remove sauteed onions and mushrooms from pan, add 1 T butter and sear lamb chops for about 5 minutes on each side.
5. Slice 1 garlic clove into pan with chops after they have been turned once.
6. When chops are seared on both sides, transfer from pan into large casserole, cover with onions and mushrooms, and pour bouillon over all. Sprinkle with 1 T chopped parsley.
7. Cover and place in oven. Set timer for 25 minutes.
8. Prepare Melba sauce by pressing raspberries through a strainer into a small saucepan.
9. Stir in sugar and cream of tartar; heat quickly to boiling and boil for about 2 1/2 minutes, stirring rapidly. Cover and chill.
10. When casserole is removed from oven, partner will add peas. Serve right from casserole.

Index

FOREIGN NIGHT IN